The lilting house

The lilting house

An anthology of Anglo–Welsh poetry 1917–67

Editors **John Stuart Williams** and **Meic Stephens**

with an introduction by Raymond Garlick

J M Dent & Sons Limited
Christopher Davies Limited

Made in Great Britain at the
Aldine Press Letchworth Hertfordshire
for J M Dent & Sons Limited
Aldine House Bedford Street London
and Christopher Davies *publishers* Limited
Llandybie Ammanford Carmarthenshire
First published 1969

Published with the support of
the Welsh Arts Council

SBN: 460 04903 8

i
Keidrych Rhys
arloeswr

ac er côf am
Vernon Watkins
1906 – 67
y mwyaf yn ein mysg

Contents

Contents

Contents

Contents

Contents

Editors' note

The beginning and the end of the period from which we have selected the poems in this anthology were marked by the publication in 1917 of *Welsh Poets*, edited by A. G. Prys-Jones, and of *Welsh Voices*, edited by Bryn Griffiths in 1967 – the year of Vernon Watkins's death and the year in which we began the compilation of this book. We have tried to represent the major Anglo-Welsh poets of the last fifty years and, at the same time, to bring to notice a number of lesser figures who have contributed to Anglo-Welsh literature in this century. Only one poet has been omitted with regret: Emyr Humphreys, who takes such strong objection to the term Anglo-Welsh that he will not allow any of his work to be published under this heading. It happens that the youngest poets who appear here were in their thirtieth year in 1967. Since then, a number of poets in their twenties have begun to make their names, but we were obliged to exclude them for the sake of keeping this book within reasonable proportions.

The publishers wish to thank the Welsh Arts Council (*Cyngor Celfyddydau Cymru*) for its generous financial assistance in the publication of this volume.

Our thanks are due to Mr Glyn Jones, Mr Aneirin Talfan Davies, Professor George Thomas and Mr Gerald Morgan for their advice in the compilation of this anthology; to Mr Raymond Garlick for his valuable introduction; to Miss Fay Williams and Mr Geraint Jarman for helping to prepare the typescript; to the trustees of the Dylan Thomas Estate for permission to use a quotation from the poem *Fern Hill* as our title and to Mr Terence Hawkes who used the same quotation as the title of an anthology of verse by students at the University College of Wales, Cardiff (Fortune Press, 1955).

Acknowledgments are also due to the poets, editors and publishers who have kindly given permission for poems to be republished here; first of all, to the editors of the principal Anglo-Welsh literary magazines: Mr Keidrych Rhys, editor of *Wales* (1939–49 and 1958–

1959); Professor Gwyn Jones, editor of *The Welsh Review* (1938–48); Mr Raymond Garlick, editor of *Dock Leaves* (1949–60); Mr Roland Mathias, editor of *The Anglo-Welsh Review*, formerly *Dock Leaves*; Mr Meic Stephens, editor of *Poetry Wales*, also to the editors of the four major anthologies of Anglo-Welsh poetry already published, Mr A. G. Prys-Jones, editor of *Welsh Poets*, (Macdonald, 1917), Mr Keidrych Rhys, editor of *Modern Welsh Poetry* (Faber, 1944), Mr Bryn Griffiths, editor of *Welsh Voices* (Dent, 1967), and Mr Gerald Morgan, editor of *This World of Wales* (University of Wales Press, 1968); then to the following: the Wesleyan University Press, Jonathan Cape Ltd and Mrs H. M. Davies for poems by W. H. Davies; Faber and Faber Ltd and Mrs Myfanwy Thomas for poems by Edward Thomas; Mrs Ann Menai Williams for poems by Huw Menai; Christopher Davies Ltd for poems by A. G. Prys-Jones; Faber and Faber Ltd for poems by Wyn Griffith; the Chilmark Press, Faber and Faber Ltd and *Agenda* for poems by David Jones; Faber and Faber Ltd for poems by Gwyn Williams; J. M. Dent and Sons Ltd, Faber and Faber Ltd and Mrs E. Davies for poems by Idris Davies; the Fortune Press, J. M. Dent and Sons Ltd, New Directions Inc. for poems by Glyn Jones; Faber and Faber Ltd and Mrs Gwen Watkins for poems by Vernon Watkins; Outposts Publications for poems by Tom Earley; the Oxford University Press for poems by Brenda Chamberlain; Rupert Hart-Davis Ltd for poems by R. S. Thomas; the trustees of the Dylan Thomas Estate and J. M. Dent and Sons Ltd for poems by Dylan Thomas; George Allen and Unwin Ltd and Mrs Gweno Lewis for poems by Alun Lewis; Putnam and Co. Ltd, the Dock Leaves Press, the Triskel Press and J. M. Dent and Sons Ltd for poems by Roland Mathias; the Triskel Press and Galerie Karl Flinker for the poem by Cyril Hodges; George Routledge Ltd for poems by Keidrych Rhys; Faber and Faber Ltd for poems by Nigel Heseltine; the Triskel Press and J. M. Dent and Sons Ltd for poems by Harri Webb; Christopher Davies Ltd and J. M. Dent and Sons Ltd for poems by John Stuart Williams; Rupert Hart-Davis Ltd and Mrs Madeleine Jones for poems by T. H. Jones; Chatto and Windus Ltd and *The Atlantic Monthly* for poems by Leslie Norris; Faber and Faber Ltd and Mrs Mary Treece for poems by Henry Treece; the Triskel Press, Rupert Hart-Davis Ltd and J. M. Dent and Sons Ltd for the poem by Robert Morgan; the Dock Leaves Press for the poem by Peter Hellings; Hutchinson and Co. Ltd and J. M. Dent and Sons Ltd for poems by Dannie Abse; the Triskel Press for poems by John Ormond; the Triskel Press for the poem by Alison J. Bielski; the Dock Leaves Press and Gwasg Gomer for poems by Raymond Garlick; the Triskel Press and J. M. Dent and Sons Ltd for poems by John Tripp; the Triskel Press for the poem by Douglas Phillips; Christopher Davies Ltd, the Triskel Press and Penguin Books Ltd for poems and translations by Anthony Conran; the Triskel Press and J. M. Dent and Sons Ltd for poems by Herbert Williams; Christopher Davies Ltd and J. M. Dent and Sons Ltd for poems by Bryn Griffiths; the Triskel Press, J. M. Dent and Sons Ltd and *The Observer* for poems by Peter Gruffydd; J. M. Dent and Sons Ltd, Cardiff Corporation and *The Poetry Review* for poems by Sally Roberts; the Dock Leaves Press for the poem by Peter Preece; the Triskel Press for poems by Alun Rees; Faber and Faber Ltd for the poem by Lynette Roberts; John Jones Ltd for poems by John Idris Jones; the Triskel Press and J. M. Dent and Sons Ltd for poems by Meic Stephens.

John Stuart Williams and Meic Stephens

Rhiwbina, Cardiff.

Introduction

As a bilingual country, Wales possesses two literatures. Anglo-Welsh literature is the creative writing of Welshmen in the English language. The convenient epithet Anglo-Welsh (which first appears, though with a non-literary application, in a footnote to a poem published in Carmarthen in 1772) makes no more than a linguistic distinction, Welsh literature being properly that magnificent body of writing – ancient as the sub-Roman age and modern as today – whose medium is the older language of Wales. As a term of literary criticism, Anglo-Welsh implies no reflection upon the Welshness of the writers in question.

Anglo-Welsh poetry is the product of a bilingual Wales, and bilingual Wales began with the Tudors – though for a long while, of course, the Welsh and not the English language was the dominant one. In this situation the Anglo-Welsh poet had a choice of roles. He might elect to interpret a largely Welsh-speaking Wales to the non-Welsh reader. 'I speake for those whose Tongues are strange to thee,' writes John Davies in 1603, to an English prince. Or he might address the limited bilingual readership within Wales, as do the English poems of Morgan Llwyd (1619–1659). The readers were the same kind of people as the writers – ministers of religion, professional men, country gentry, and it is for this reason that the language of Anglo-Welsh poetry has been, with few exceptions, a standard and not a dialectal English.

It seems probable that about a hundred Welshmen published poetry in English between the end of the sixteenth century and the beginning of the twentieth – many of them bilingual, most of them no doubt of interest only to the student. However, literatures do not spring into existence fully formed, like Athena from the head of Zeus – which they forget who would attribute to Anglo-Welsh literature some arbitrary date of origin a mere forty or fifty years ago. In the mysterious economy of poetry – whereby it seems that for the few to be chosen, many must be called – the archive of minor Anglo-Welsh versifiers down the centuries has a cumulative significance. To what extent they were aware of each other is uncertain, though there can be little question of a conscious tradition until the present century. On the other hand, there is a recurrence of themes – the past, Welsh myth and history, Welsh landscape, the two languages – and of technical preoccupations, particularly aural and visual ones, which link them with some of the poets in this anthology. Relationships between Welsh and Anglo-Welsh literature have been little investigated, but obviously they are involved in any complete reading of David Jones, Glyn Jones, R. S. Thomas, Anthony Conran and some others.

The industrialization of south Wales and the introduction of compulsory English-language education in the nineteenth century, and in the twentieth such factors as compulsory military service, the decline of Welsh Nonconformity, the very extensive use of English in higher education, and the revolutions in transport and communications, have reversed the balance of the languages of Wales. The contemporary voices in this book are raised in a Wales for two-thirds of whose population English is the mother tongue.

These changes have increased the numbers, the readers and the responsibilities of Anglo-Welsh poets, and have clarified the poet's role. During the earlier decades of the present century his eye rolled in a mild frenzy, glancing from London to Wales, from Wales to London, in some cases via the United States of America. The latitude which the interpretative position could allow itself is best typified in the ebullience of Dylan Thomas – of whom Saunders Lewis has written that he treated everything, including the English language, as a plaything granted by God to His children, the poets. That the role was not to be dismissed as frivolous he made clear when he went on to describe this poet as the most splendid English-speaking child Wales had produced for centuries.

In more recent years, however, the other role of the Anglo-Welsh poet – reciprocal rather than interpretative – has come into its own. Asked (as early as 1946) for whom he wrote, R. S. Thomas quoted Yeats's quatrain:

> All day I'd looked in the face
> What I had hoped 'twould be
> To write for my own race
> And the reality.

A considerable number of the poets represented in this anthology mirror this sober statement of intention. What all the poems communicate – however much or little it may at first appear to have to do with Wales – is Welsh in the sense that it is being presented by a sensibility which (through heredity, or environment, or both) is not English, though it shapes the English language to its own purposes. All of them are Welsh in that they are ultimately statements about what it is like to be a Welsh human being. But some of them are Welsh in this fullest sense, that not only are they written by Welshmen or about Wales – they are written for Wales: in other words, they do not differ in intention from poems written in the Welsh language. This is the Anglo-Welsh statement in its most complete form. There are some to whom it may seem wilfully narrow. Yet it is precisely this steady gaze at one clearly defined acre of the experience of Europe, under the dimensions of space and time, that has drawn to some of these poems (by the paradox whereby the more particularly a thing is observed, the more universal its appeal) a readership far beyond the borders of Wales.

If there have been moments in the past when the Anglo-Welsh poet has seemed to play Esau to the Welsh poet's Jacob, in the sixties the cohering of the sense of national identity in all sections of Welsh life has kindled a vocation of reconciliation among writers, the most articulate members of the language communities – a concern for unity in bilingualism, an awareness of the one, whole Wales, which also (like Whitman) embraces contradictions and multitudes. This has been reflected in the opening of Anglo-Welsh lists by Welsh publishers, the study of Anglo-Welsh texts in some schools and colleges (academic interest abroad, notably in German and French universities, is long-standing), and the establishment of an Anglo-Welsh section by Yr Academi Gymreig, the Academy of Letters. It is also to be seen in the publication of such books as Bryn Griffiths's *Welsh Voices* (Dent, 1967), Gerald Morgan's *This World of Wales* (University of Wales Press, 1968), and Glyn Jones's *The Dragon has Two Tongues* (Dent, 1968). Fifty years after the 1917 anthology of A. G. Prys-Jones, the present book sets out to offer the authoritative, comprehensive and representative twentieth-century anthology which has long been lacking.

Raymond Garlick,
Trinity College, Carmarthen.

W. H. Davies   1871 - 1940

Come, honest boys

Ye who have nothing to conceal,
    Come, honest boys, and drink with me;
Come, drink with me the sparkling ale,
    And we'll not whisper calumny,
But laugh with all the power we can;
    But all pale schemers who incline
To rise above your fellow man,
    Touch not the sparkling ale or wine.

Give me strong ale to fire my blood,
    Content me with a lot that's bad;
That is to me both drink and food,
    And warms me though I am ill-clad;
A pot of ale, man owns the world:
    The poet hears his songs all sung,
Inventor sees his patents sold,
    The painter sees his pictures hung.

The creeds remind us oft of Death;
    But man's best creed is to forget
Death all the hours that he takes breath,
    And quaff the sparkling ale, and let
Creeds shout until they burst their lungs;
    For what is better than to be
A-drinking ale and singing songs,
    In summer, under some green tree?

The collier's wife

The collier's wife had four tall sons
   Brought from the pit's mouth dead,
   And crushed from foot to head;
When others brought her husband home,
Had five dead bodies in her room.

Had five dead bodies in her house –
   All in a row they lay –
   To bury in one day:
Such sorrow in the valley has
Made kindness grow like grass.

Oh, collier, collier, underground,
   In fear of fire and gas,
   What life more danger has?
Who fears more danger in this life?
There is but one – thy wife!

The kingfisher

It was the Rainbow gave thee birth,
   And left thee all her lovely hues;
And, as her mother's name was Tears,
   So runs it in my blood to choose
For haunts the lonely pools, and keep
In company with trees that weep.

Go you and, with such glorious hues,
    Live with proud Peacocks in green parks;
On lawns as smooth as shining glass,
    Let every feather show its marks;
Get thee on boughs and clap thy wings
Before the windows of proud kings.

Nay, lovely Bird, thou art not vain;
    Thou hast no proud, ambitious mind;
I also love a quiet place
    That's green, away from all mankind;
A lonely pool, and let a tree
Sigh with her bosom over me.

Days that have been

Can I forget the sweet days that have been,
    When poetry first began to warm my blood;
When from the hills of Gwent I saw the earth
    Burned into two by Severn's silver flood;

When I would go alone at night to see
    The moonlight, like a big white butterfly,
Dreaming on that old castle near Caerleon,
    While at its side the Usk went softly by:

When I would stare at lovely clouds in Heaven,
    Or watch them when reported by deep streams;
When feeling pressed like thunder, but would not
    Break into that grand music of my dreams?

Can I forget the sweet days that have been,
  The villages so green I have been in;
Llantarnam, Magor, Malpas, and Llanwern,
  Liswery, old Caerleon, and Alteryn?

Can I forget the banks of Malpas Brook,
  Or Ebbw's voice in such a wild delight,
As on he dashed with pebbles in his throat,
  Gurgling towards the sea with all his might?

Ah, when I see a leafy village now,
  I sigh and ask it for Llantarnam's green;
I ask each river where is Ebbw's voice –
  In memory of the sweet days that have been.

Edward Thomas   1878 - 1917

Words

Out of us all
That make rhymes,
Will you choose
Sometimes –
As the winds use
A crack in a wall
Or a drain,
Their joy or their pain
To whistle through –
Choose me,
You English words?

I know you:
You are light as dreams,
Tough as oak,
Precious as gold,
As poppies and corn,
Or an old cloak:
Sweet as our birds
To the ear,
As the burnet rose
In the heat
Of Midsummer:
Strange as the races
Of dead and unborn:
Strange and sweet
Equally,
And familiar,
To the eye,
As the dearest faces
That a man knows,

And as lost homes are:
But though older far
Than oldest yew, –
As our hills are, old, –
Worn new
Again and again:
Young as our streams
After rain:
And as dear
As the earth which you prove
That we love.

Make me content
With some sweetness
From Wales
Whose nightingales
Have no wings, –
From Wiltshire and Kent
And Herefordshire,
And the villages there, –
From the names, and the things
No less.
Let me sometimes dance
With you,
Or climb
Or stand perchance
In ecstasy,
Fixed and free
In a rhyme,
As poets do.

The owl

Downhill I came, hungry, and yet not starved;
Cold, yet had heat within me that was proof
Against the North wind; tired, yet so that rest
Had seemed the sweetest thing under a roof.

Then at the inn I had food, fire, and rest,
Knowing how hungry, cold, and tired was I.
All of the night was quite barred out except
An owl's cry, a most melancholy cry

Shaken out long and clear upon the hill,
No merry note, nor cause of merriment,
But one telling me plain what I escaped
And others could not, that night, as in I went.

And salted was my food, and my repose,
Salted and sobered, too, by the bird's voice
Speaking for all who lay under the stars,
Soldiers and poor, unable to rejoice.

It rains

It rains, and nothing stirs within the fence
Anywhere through the orchard's untrodden, dense
Forest of parsley. The great diamonds
Of rain on the grassblades there is none to break,
Or the fallen petals further down to shake.

And I am nearly as happy as possible
To search the wilderness in vain though well,
To think of two walking, kissing there,
Drenched, yet forgetting the kisses of the rain:
Sad, too, to think that never, never again,

Unless alone, so happy shall I walk
In the rain. When I turn away, on its fine stalk
Twilight has fined to naught, the parsley flower
Figures, suspended still and ghostly white,
The past hovering as it revisits the light.

Roads

I love roads:
The goddesses that dwell
Far along invisible
Are my favourite gods.

Roads go on
While we forget, and are
Forgotten like a star
That shoots and is gone.

On this earth 'tis sure
We men have not made
Anything that doth fade
So soon, so long endure:

The hill road wet with rain
In the sun would not gleam
Like a winding stream
If we trod it not again.

They are lonely
While we sleep, lonelier
For lack of the traveller
Who is now a dream only.

From dawn's twilight
And all the clouds like sheep
On the mountains of sleep
They wind into the night.

The next turn may reveal
Heaven: upon the crest
The close pine clump, at rest
And black, may Hell conceal.

Often footsore, never
Yet of the road I weary,
Though long and steep and dreary,
As it winds on for ever.

Helen of the roads,
The mountain ways of Wales
And the Mabinogion tales
Is one of the true gods,

Abiding in the trees,
The threes and fours so wise,
The larger companies,
That by the roadside be,

And beneath the rafter
Else uninhabited
Excepting by the dead;
And it is her laughter

At morn and night I hear
When the thrush cock sings
Bright irrelevant things,
And when the chanticleer

Calls back to their own night
Troops that make loneliness
With their light footsteps' press,
As Helen's own are light.

Now all roads lead to France
And heavy is the tread
Of the living; but the dead
Returning lightly dance:

Whatever the road bring
To me or take from me,
They keep me company
With their pattering,

Crowding the solitude
Of the loops over the downs,
Hushing the roar of towns
And their brief multitude.

Tall nettles

Tall nettles cover up, as they have done
These many springs, the rusty harrow, the plough
Long worn out, and the roller made of stone:
Only the elm butt tops the nettles now.

This corner of the farmyard I like most:
As well as any bloom upon a flower
I like the dust on the nettles, never lost
Except to prove the sweetness of a shower.

Lights out

I have come to the borders of sleep,
The unfathomable deep
Forest where all must lose
Their way, however straight,
Or winding, soon or late;
They cannot choose.

Many a road and track
That, since the dawn's first crack,
Up to the forest brink,
Deceived the travellers,
Suddenly now blurs,
And in they sink.

Here love ends,
Despair, ambition ends;
All pleasure and all trouble,
Although most sweet or bitter,
Here ends in sleep that is sweeter
Than tasks most noble.

There is not any book
Or face of dearest look
That I would not turn from now
To go into the unknown
I must enter, and leave, alone,
I know not how.

The tall forest towers;
Its cloudy foliage lowers
Ahead, shelf above shelf;
Its silence I hear and obey
That I may lose my way
And myself.

Huw Menai   1887 - 1961

Cwm farm near Capel Curig

Some cool medieval calm hath settled here
   On this lone farmstead, wherein humble folk
   Still speak the tongue that Owain Glyndŵr spoke,
And worship in it, too, the God they fear.
For to these perilous Ways, where rocks rise sheer,
   Their kinsmen came to curse the tyrant yoke;
   And here the proud invader's heart was broke
By brave and stubborn men year after year.
Unconquerable still! here birds but know
   The Cymric speech; the very mountains brood
O'er consonants that, rugged streamlets, flow
   Into deep vowel lakes . . . and by this wood,
   Where Prince Llywelyn might himself have stood,
Forget-me-nots in wild profusion grow!

The old peasant in the billiard saloon

Stretched out full length, his eighty years too ripe
　For upright posture, on the bench each day
Sleeping aloud, or tugging at his pipe,
　Or one eye open on the billiard play.
A sufferer from old age too wise for tears!
　And does he see, in that smoke-ridden place,
Th' Almighty Cueist sending the different spheres
　Upon their business spinning through all space?
Or does it make for a more homely scene,
　With him a lusty youth in Somerset
Bringing the cattle home through fields of green?
　Muttering of something that he has not met!
　Muttering to himself, his later sense
　Having found none worthier of his confidence!

A. G. Prys-Jones b. 1888

A ballad of Glyn Dŵr's rising

My son, the mist is clearing and the moon will soon be high,
And then we'll hear the thudding hooves, the horsemen speeding by,
With murmurs coming nearer, carried over on the breeze
Of the men who march in secret through the cloisters of the trees:
Tonight we two go riding, for the threads of fate are spun,
And we join Glyn Dŵr at Corwen at the rising of the sun.

For yesterday our leader was proclaimed the Prince of Wales,
His call to arms is sounding now among the hills and vales,
And Owain, heir of dynasties, in this auspicious year
May be our great deliverer, foretold by bard and seer:
And rumour runs that Arthur's voice is heard along the west
Acclaiming this descendant of Cadwaladr the Blest.

At last shall I unsheath again my father's two-edged sword,
And hand you mine to strike amain at Ruthin's tyrant lord,
Because I've waited, waited long throughout the bitter years
For this hour of freedom's challenge and the flashing of the spears:
So now we two must face as one the hazards of the night
To pledge our lives to Owain at the breaking of the light.

My son, go kiss your mother, kiss her gently, she'll not wake,
For an older mother calls you, though you perish for her sake:
The fabled Dragon banner flies once more above the Dee
Where the sons of Wales are gathering to set our people free
From wrong and dire oppression: pray, my son for strength anew,
For widows will be weeping at the falling of the dew.

Salt marshes

These marsh-lands make for sorrow:
I can feel
The ancient grief of grass, the gloom of water,
The menace of those potent, unseen powers
That ride their wings of dread to hag the dark.
See how that witch the twilight hurrying here
Makes sharp her sickle-edge to mow the day;
And how the ragged mendicants of mist
In shifty garb rise up from stealthy lairs
Thrusting their shapeless hands about your face,
Obtruding, clammy, obdurate and clinging.

The sun has set: the tide warps trembling in,
Muting its rhymes and cadences:
The black dykes gurgle like small children choking
In quick convulsions, speechless and afraid,
And, overall, the blind shapes of the sheep
Move in a muffled mob to shelter.

This is no place for mortals,
It is anguished ground, and, maybe, Cain-accursed,
Barren and boorish in its bitter days
And pagan in its vows of eldritch evil;
Unhallowed grave for seamen's flotsam bones
Picked white by plucking seas,
And sepulchre of shreds of winnowed ships
That once wove heraldry upon the waves
In coloured flight, uncaged by silting sands.

Yet I was comforted when I discerned,
Like a white nun within a lazar-house,
The blessed candle of a gentle spirit
Drawn to this shore by some strong cord of love:
And knew, with her oblations made and ended,
Redemption pouring in on shriven tides.

A day which endures not

As for me
I have seen Llywelyn
With all the valiant men of Wales around him,
His armies like the hosts of Merfyn;
And have marched with chieftains mustering
On the steep hills and the deep lowlands,
Pillars of war were they all, and mighty.

I have seen brave youth in battle
And heard the high thunder of horsemen:
I have drunk rare wines from chalices,
With rich meats laid on fine linen
In the bountiful palaces of princes.

I have listened to much oratory,
To the jewelled harmonies of bards
Declaiming their lyrics in intricate metres:
I have heard the songs and satires
Of itinerant minstrels,
And shared the merriment of maidens
Tickled by the saucy tales of story-tellers.

I have had my fill also
Of festivals and ceremonies,
The gleam and glitter of contests
Where strong men rejoiced in their prowess
And the clever in their cunning.

But now all these are gone
Like dreams in the morning:
And thus, each soul must journey forth
At the time of his reckoning
From a day which endures not:
In this the lord of many lands
The poor man's master
Gains no reprieve, no respite:
He passes through the portal with the peasant.

Adapted from the Welsh of Elidr Sais, thirteenth century.

Quite so

Within the whispering gallery of St Paul's
The merest whisper travels round the walls:
But in the parts where I was born and bred
Folk hear things long before they're even said.

Business as usual

When Gabriel's starting trumpet rends the skies,
And all arise for that last race of man,
Dai Jones, the bookie, glasses to his eyes,
Will spot the winners, and the also-ran.

Spring comes to Glamorgan

To-day I saw Spring's footprints in the Vale,
Small snowdrops glistening in a dawn-green dell
Beyond Llysworney:
And then, towards the sea,
Below St Hilary, where thrush-song rings,
I heard her trysting-call fall through the trees
Within the primrose wood where Merlin flings
His saffron mantle to the daffodils.

To-day, I saw grey tombstones hoar with moss
In deep St Donat's where the Stradlings sleep
Between their rock-fast castle-keep
And the soft lowland.
And there I saw the carven Crucified
Upon His Calvary Cross:
He did not stir, for all His suffering;
Nor moved the marble angels from their places
To quench His endless agony.

But they that lay so long with upturned faces,
Each in his narrow niche of this rich earth
Within the sanctuary of the lichened wall,
These all
Had heard Spring's call,
And woken from their oaken sleeping.
And so they pass
Along the old, familiar pathways of the grass
Towards the woods where birds are music making,
Where crocuses are breaking:
They come, these visitants, with arms outspread;
No bonds of wood and clay
Can keep them captive here on such a day:
On such a day as this along the Vale
There are no dead.

Wyn Griffith   b. 1890

Silver jubilee

Faint now in the evening pallor
answering nothing but old cries,
a troop of men shouldering their way
with a new tune I recognize

as something near to Flanders, but far
from the dragon years we killed
to no purpose, scattered seed
on land none but the devil tilled.

That a poet sings as his heart beats
is no new word, but an ancient tale.
Grey shadows on the pavement
and Europe sick of its own bale.

I have no answer, no rising song
to the young in years who are old
with our arrogance, our failure.
Let it be silence: the world is cold.

Poem

If there be time enough before the slaughter
let us consider our heritage
of wisdom, remembering the coil of laughter
girdled our youth, wine of bright vintage
carrying short sorrows into oblivion;
some talk of love in smooth meadows
where dusk brings quiet and night a vision
of daylight joys freed from their shadows.
Above all, wisdom: for years are shrinking
into a huddle of days and the world a parish
where neighbours bolt their doors and lights are dimming.
Soon there will be nothing left for us to cherish
but the grave words of the last statesmen
before the battle starts and the air is darkened:
fast falls the night upon the frightened children
and on the wombs where once they quickened.
What towered land of man's endeavour
will first be desert, with all our learning
a burnt page trodden in the dust of error?
Farewell to wisdom and to all remembering.

David Jones   b. 1895

The wall

We don't know the ins and outs
   how should we? how could we?
It's not for the likes of you and me to cogitate high policy or to guess the
inscrutable economy of the pontifex
   from the circuit of the agger
   from the traverse of the wall.
But you see a thing or two
   in our walk of life
   walking the compass of the vallum
walking for twenty years of nights
   round and round and back & fro
on the walls that contain the world.

You see a thing or two, you think a thing or two, in our walk of life, walking
for twenty years, by day, by night, doing the rounds on the walls that maintain
the world

   on the hard tread of the silex
   on the heavy tread of the mound
up in the traversed out-work, stepping it at the alert, down on the *via
quintana* stepping it double-quick by numbers to break y'r tiro-heart . . .
   dug in wrong side the *limes*
or walled in back at depot?

                                  it's evens, more or less
   as far as jumping to it goes.

But what about the Omphalos

there's the place for the proud walkers

    where the terminal gate

    arcs for the sections in column

stepping their extra fancy step

    behind the swag and spolia

o' the universal world

                  . . . out from The Camp

in through the dexter arch of double-wayed Carmenta

by where Aventine flanks The Circus

           (from Arx the birds deploy?)

to where the totem mother

        imported

        Ionian

        of bronze

brights Capitoline for ever

           (from the Faunine slope of creviced Palatine does the grey wraith erect her throat to welcome the lupine gens?)

Erect, crested with the open fist that turns the evil spell, lifting the flat palm that disciplines the world, the signa lift in disciplined acknowledgement, the eagles stand erect for Ilia

        O Roma

        O Ilia

        Io Triumphe, Io, Io . . .

        the shopkeepers presume to make

the lupine cry their own

           the magnates of the Boarium leave their nice manipulations. You may call the day ferial, rub shoulders with the plebs. All should turn out to see how those appointed to die take the Roman medicine. They crane their civvy necks half out their civvy suits to bait the maimed king in his tinctured vesture, the dying *tegernos* of the wasted *landa* well webbed in our marbled parlour, bitched and bewildered and far from his dappled patria far side the misted Fretum.

You can think a thing or two

on *that* parade:

    Do the celestial forechoosings
    and the hard journeyings

come to this?

    Did the empyreal fires

hallow the chosen womb

    to tabernacle founders of
    emporia?

Were the august conjoinings

    was the troia'd wandering
    achieved

did the sallow ducts of Luperca

    nourish the lily white boys

was Electra chose

    from the seven stars in the sky

did Ilia bear fruit to the Strider
    was she found the handmaid of the Lar

did the augurs inaugurate, did the Clarissimi steady the transverse rods, did they align the plummets carefully, did they check the bearing attentively, was the templum dead true at the median intersection

    did the white unequal pair
labour the yoke, tread the holy circuit

    did they, so early

in the marls of Cispadana

    show forth, foretoken

the rudiments of our order

    when the precursors at the
valley-sites made survey of the loam, plotted the trapezoids on the sodden piles, digged the sacred pits, before the beginning . . .

    did they square the hill-sites for the
hut-circles, did the hill-groups look to each other, were the hostile strong-points one by one, made co-ordinate

    did Quirinal with Viminal

call to the Quadrata
                    did the fence of Tullius
embrace the mixed kindreds
did the magic wall
                    (that keeps the walls)
describe the orbit
did that wall contain a world
                    from the beginning
did they project the rectilineal plane upwards
to the floor of heaven
had all
            within that reaching prism
                    one patria:
                    rooted clod or drifted star
                    dog or dryad or
                    man born of woman
did the sacred equation square the mundane site
was truth with fact conjoined
                    did the earth-mother
blossom the stone lintels
                    did *urvus* become *urbs*
did the bright share
                    turn the dun clod
to the star plan   did they parcel out
per scamna et strigas
                    the *civitas* of God
that we should sprawl
                    from Septimontium
a megalopolis that wills death?

Does the pontifex, do our lifted trumpets, speak to the city and the world to
call the tribes to Saturnalia to set misrule in the curule chair, to bind the
rejected fillet on the King of the Bean?

          It's hard to trapes these things
from the circuit of the agger
from the traverse of the wall
          waiting for the middle watch to pass
wanting the guard-house fug
          where the companions nod
          where the sooted billikin
brews the night broth

          so cold it is, so numb the intelligence, so chancy
the intuition, so alert the apprehension for us who walk in darkness, in the
shadow of the *onager*, in the shadow of the labyrinth of the wall, of the world,
of the robber walls of the world city, trapesing the macrocosmic night.
Or, trapesing the night within, walking the inner labyrinth where also the night
is, under the tortoise of the skull, for every man walking?
Under the legionary's iron knob, under the tribune's field crest, under the
very distinguished gilt *cassis* of the Legatus himself?
          We don't know the ins and outs
how can we? how shall we?
What did our mothers tell us? What did their mothers tell them? What the
earth-mother told to them? But what did the queen of heaven tell *her*?
What was it happened by the fire-flame eating the griddle-cake . . . or by the
white porch where our sister sang the Sabine dirge.

. . . they used to say we marched for Dea Roma behind the wolf sign to eat
up the world, they used to say we marched for the Strider, the common father
of the Roman people, the father of all in our walk of life, by whose very name
you're called. . . .

but now they say the Quirinal Mars turns out to be no god of war but of armed peace. Now they say we march for kind Irene, who crooks her rounded elbow for little Plutus, the gold-getter, and they say that sacred brat has a future . . .

> now all can face the dying god
> the dying Gaul
> without regret.

But you and me, comrade, the Darlings of Ares, who've helped a lot of Gauls and god to die, we shall continue to march and to bear in our bodies the marks of the Marcher – by whatever name they call him . . .

> we shall continue to march
> round and round the cornucopia:

that's the new fatigue.

The sleeping lord (extract)

Tawny-black sky-scurries
         low over
Ysgyryd hill
and over the level-topped heights
         of Mynydd Pen-y-fal
         cold is wind
         grey is rain, but
         BRIGHT IS CANDELA
where this lord is in slumber.

Are his wounded ankles
         lapped with the ferric waters
that all through the night
         hear the song
from the night-dark seams
         where the narrow-skulled *caethion*
labour the changing shifts
         for the cosmocrats of alien lips
in all the fair lands
         of the dark measures under
from about Afon Lwyd
         in the confines of green Siluria
westward to where the naïad of the *fons*-head
         pours out the Lesser Gwendraeth
high in the uplands
         above Ystrad Tywi
and indeed further
         west and south of Merlin's Caer
even in the lost cantrevs
         of spell-held Demetia
where was Gorsedd Arberth, where the *palas,* was
         where the prince who hunted
met the Prince of Hunters

         in his woof of grey
and gleam-pale dogs
         not kennelled on earth-floor

lit the dim chase.
Is the Usk a drain for his gleaming tears
who weeps for the land
                who dreams his bitter dream
for the folk of the land
does Tawe clog for his sorrows
do the parallel dark-seam drainers
                mingle his anguish-stream
with the scored valleys' tilted refuse.
Does his freight of woe
                flood South by East
on Sirhywi and Ebwy
                is it southly bourn
on double Rhondda's fall to Taff?

  Do the stripped boughs grapple
above the troubled streams
                when he dream-fights
his nine-days' fight
                which he fought alone
with the hog in the Irish wilderness
                when the eighteen twilights
                and the ten midnights
and the equal light of the nine mid-mornings
were equally lit
                with the light of the saviour's fury
and the dark fires of the hog's eye
which encounter availed him nothing.
                Is his royal anger ferriaged
where black-rimed Rhymni
                soils her Marcher-banks
                Do the bells of St Mellon's
toll his dolour
                are his sighs canalled
where the mountain-ash
                droops her bright head
for the black pall of Merthyr?

Do Afan and Nedd west it away
does grimed Ogwr toss on a fouled ripple
his broken-heart flow
　　　　　　out to widening Hafren
　　　　　　and does she, the Confluence Queen
queenly bear on her spume-frilled frock
a maimed king's sleep bane?
　　　　　　Do the long white hands
would you think, of the Brides of the Déssi
　　　　　　unloose galloons
to let the black tress-stray
　　　　　　web the pluvial Westerlies
does the vestal flame in virid-hilled Kildare
　　　　　　renew from secret embers
the undying fire
　　　　　　that sinks on the Hill Capitoline
　Does the wake-dole mingle the cormorant scream
does man-*sidhe* to fay-queen bemoan
the passage of a king's griefs, westing far
　　　　　　out to moon-swayed Oceanus
　Does the blind & unchoosing creature of sea know the marking and
indelible balm from flotsomed sewage and the seaped valley-waste?
Does the tide-beast's maw
　　　　　　drain down the princely tears
with the mullocked slag-wash
　　　　　　of Special Areas?
Can the tumbling and gregarious porpoises
does the aloof and infrequent seal
　　　　　　that suns his puckered back
　　　　　　and barks from Pirus' rock
tell the dole-tally of a drowned *taeog* from a
Gwledig's golden collar, refracted in Giltar shoal?

Or, is the dying gull
               on her sea-hearse
that drifts the oily bourne
               to tomb at turn of tide
her own stricken cantor?
Or is it for the royal tokens
               that with her drift
that the jagg'd and jutting *morben* echoes
and the deep hollows of *yr ogof* echo
and the hollow eddies echo:
               Dirige, dirige
and out, far, far beyond
on thalassic Brendan's heaving trackway
to unknown *insulae*
               where they sing
their west In Paradisums
               and the corposants toss
for the dying flax-flame
               and West-world glory
in transit is.

But yet he sleeps:
               when he shifts a little in his fitful slumber
does a covering stone dislodge
               and roll to Reynoldstone?
When he fretfully turns
               crying out in a great voice
               in his fierce sleep-anger
does the habergeon'd sentinel
               alert himself sudden
from his middle-watch doze
               in the crenelled traverse-bay
of the outer bailey wall
               of the *castell* these Eingel-Ffrancwyr
call in their lingua La Haie Taillée
that the Saeson other ranks
               call The Hay
(which place is in the tongue of the men of the land,
Y Gelli Gandryll, or for short, Y Gelli)

Does he cock his weather-ear, enquiringly
lest what's on the west wind
               from over beyond the rising contours
may signify that in the broken
        tir y blaenau
these broken dregs of Troea
           yet again muster?
Does he nudge his drowsing mate?
          Do the pair of them
say to each other: 'Twere not other
than wind-cry, for sure – yet
            best to warn the serjeant below.
He'll maybe
           warn the Captain of the Watch
or some such
          and he, as like as not
may think best to rouse the Castellan
         – that'll please him
in his newly glazed, arras-hung chamber
          with his Dean-coal fire
nicely blazing
snug with his dowsabel
          in the inner keep.
Wont improve his temper, neither, come the morrow
with this borough and hereabouts alerted
         and all for but a wind-bluster.
Still, you never know, so
          best stand on Standing Orders
and report to them as has the serjeancy
the ordering and mandate, for
you never know, mate:
         wind-stir maybe, most like to be
as we between us do agree
         or – stir of gramarye
or whatsomever of ferly – who should say?
         or solid substantiality?
you never know *what* may be
         – not hereabouts.

No wiseman's son *born* do know
                not in these whoreson March-lands
of this Welshry.

Yet he sleeps on
               very deep is his slumber:
how long has he been the sleeping lord?
are the clammy ferns
               his rustling vallance
does the buried rowan
               ward him from evil, or
does he ward the tanglewood
               and the denizens of the wood
are the stunted oaks his gnarled guard
               or are their knarred limbs
strong with his sap?
Do the small black horses
               grass on the hunch of his shoulders?
are the hills his couch
               or is he the couchant hills?
Are the slumbering valleys
               him in slumber
               are the still undulations
the still limbs of him sleeping?
Is the configuration of the land
               the furrowed body of the lord
are the scarred ridges
               his dented greaves
do the trickling gullies
               yet drain his hog-wounds?
Does the land wait the sleeping lord
               or is the wasted land
that very lord who sleeps?

The boast of Dai (extract from *In Parenthesis*)

This Dai adjusts his slipping shoulder-straps, wraps close his misfit outsize greatcoat – he articulates his English with an alien care.

My fathers were with the Black Pris of Wales
at the passion of
the blind Bohemian king.
They served in these fields,
it is in the histories that you can read it, Corporal – boys. Gower, they were –
it is writ down – yes.

Wot about Methuselum, Taffy?
I was with Abel when his brother found him,
under the green tree.
I built a shit-house for Artaxerxes.
I was the spear in Balin's hand
     that made waste King Pellam's land.
I took the smooth stones of the brook,
I was with Saul
playing before him.
I saw him armed like Derfel Gatheren.
I the fox-run fire
   consuming in the wheat-lands;
and in the standing wheat in Cantium made some attempt to form – between dun August oaks their pied bodies darting. And I the south air, tossed from high projections by his Olifant; (the arid marcher-slopes echoing – should they lose
Clere Espaigne la bele).

I am '62 Socrates, my feet are colder than you think
on this
Potidaean duck-board.

I the adder in the little bush
whose hibernation-end
undid,
unmade victorious toil:
In ostium fluminis.
At the four actions in regione Linnuis
    by the black waters.
At Bassas in the shallows.

At Cat Coit Celidon.
At Guinnion redoubt, where he carried the Image.
In urbe Legionis.
By the vallum Antonini, at the place of boundaries, at the toiling estuary
and strong flow called Tribruit.
By Agned mountain.
On Bodon hill, where he bore the Tree.
  I am the Loricated Legions.
Helen Camulodunum is ours;
she's the toast of the Rig'ment,
she is in an especial way our Mediatrix.
  She's clement and loving, she's Friday's child, she's loving and giving;
O dulcis
imperatrix.
  Her ample bosom holds:
Pontifex maximus,
Comes Litoris Saxonici,
Comes Britanniarum,
Gwledig,
Bretwalda, as these square-heads say.
  She's the girl with the sparkling eyes,
she's the Bracelet Giver,
she's a regular draw with the labour companies,
whereby
the paved army-paths are hers that grid the island which is her dower.
Elen Luyddog she is – more she is than
Helen Argive.
  My mob digged the outer vallum,
we furnished picquets;
we staked trip-wire as a precaution at
Troy Novaunt.
  I saw the blessèd head set under
                that kept the narrow sea inviolate,
To keep the Land,
to give the yield:
  under the White Tower
      I trowelled the inhuming mortar.

They learned me well the proportions due –
by water
by sand
by slacked lime.
    I drest the cist –
the beneficent artisans knew well how to keep
the king's head to keep
the land inviolate.
    The Bear of the Island: he broke it in his huge pride, and over-reach of his
imperium.
The Island Dragon.
The Bull of Battle
    (this is the third woeful uncovering).
Let maimed kings lie – let be
O let the guardian head
keep back – bind savage sails, lock the shield-wall, nourish the sowing.
The War Duke
The Director of Toil –
    he burst the balm-cloth, unbricked the barrow
(cruel feet march because of this
                ungainly men sprawl over us).
O Land! – O Brân lie under.
The chrism'd eye that watches the French-men
that wards under
that keeps us
that brings the furrow-fruit,
keep the land, keep us
keep the islands adjacent.

I marched. sixty thousand and one thousand marched, because of the bright-
ness of Flur, because of the keeper of promises
    (we came no more again)
who depleted the Island,
    (and this is the first emigrant host)
and the land was bare for our going.
    O blessèd head hold the striplings from the narrow sea.
    I marched, sixty thousand marched who marched for Kunan and Elen

because of foreign machinations,
    (we came no more again)
who left the land without harness
    (and this is the second emigrant host).
O Brân confound the counsel of the councillors, O blessèd head, hold the striplings from the narrow sea.
    In the baized chamber confuse his tongue:
that Lord Agravaine.
He urges with repulsive lips, he counsels: he nets us into expeditionary war.
    O blessèd head hold the striplings‾from the narrow sea.
    I knew the smart on Branwen's cheek and the turbulence in Ireland
        (and this was the third grievous blow).
    I served Longinus that Dux bat-blind and bent;
the Dandy Xth are my regiment;
who diced
Crown and Mud-hook
under the Tree,
whose Five Sufficient Blossoms
yield for us.
    I kept the boding raven
        from the Dish.
With my long pilum
I beat the crow
from that heavy bough.
    But I held the tunics of these –
I watched them work the terrible embroidery that He put on.
I heard there, sighing for the Feet so shod.
I saw cock-robin gain
    his rosy breast.
I heard Him cry:
        Apples ben ripe in my gardayne
I saw Him die.
    I was in Michael's trench when bright Lucifer bulged his primal salient out.
That caused it,
that upset the joy-cart,
and three parts waste.

You ought to ask: Why,
what is this,
what's the meaning of this.
Because you don't ask,
although the spear-shaft
drips,
there's neither steading – not a roof-tree.
I am the Single Horn thrusting
by night-stream margin
in Helyon.

Cripes-a-mighty-strike-me-stone-cold – you don't say.
Where's that birth-mark, young 'un.
Wot the Melchizzydix! – and still fading – jump to it Rotherhithe.
Never die never die
Never die never die
Old soljers never die
Never die never die
Old soljers never die they never die
Never die
Old soljers never die they
Simply fade away.

Gwyn Williams   b. 1904

Cynddylan's hall

Cynddylan's hall is dark tonight
no fire no bed
I'll be still when these tears are shed.

Cynddylan's hall is dark tonight
no fire no taper
God's the only patience giver.

Cynddylan's hall is dark tonight
no light no fire
the grief that you inspire!

Cynddylan's hall is dark of roof
after bright company
do good if you've ability.

Cynddylan's hall has been defaced
your wall's defender
is dead your lifelong mender.

Cynddylan's hall's forlorn tonight
after its owner
O death why do you leave me here?

Cynddylan's hall is dull tonight
on Hytwyth's height
no lord no army and no might.

Cynddylan's hall is dark tonight
no fire no singing
my two cheeks waste with weeping.

Cynddylan's hall is dark tonight
no fire no household
night finds my tears uncontrolled.

Cynddylan's hall hurts me to see
no fire no wit
my chief is dead but I live yet.

Cynddylan's hall's a ruin tonight
bravest and pleasantest
Elvan Cynddylan Kaeawc rest.

Cynddylan's hall is sad tonight
after the fame it knew
gone is its numerous retinue.

Cynddylan's hall is heavy tonight
without a chieftain
great God have mercy on my pain.

No lights hang in Cynddylan's hall
since the English ruined
Cynddylan and Elvan of Powys land.

Cynddylan's hall is dark tonight
Cyndrwynyn's breed
Cynon and Gwiawn and Gwyn are dead.

Cynddylan's hall is my long pain
after the bustle
I've seen beneath its roof trestle.

Translated from the Welsh of an anonymous ninth century poet.

Eagle of Pengwern

Eagle of Pengwern, grey-crested, tonight
  its shriek is high,
    eager for flesh I loved.

Eagle of Pengwern, grey-crested, tonight
    its call is high,
    eager for Cynddylan's flesh.

Eagle of Pengwern, grey-crested, tonight
    its claw is high,
    eager for flesh I love.

Eagle of Pengwern, it called far tonight,
    it kept watch on men's blood;
  Trenn shall be called a luckless town.

Eagle of Pengwern, it calls far tonight,
    it feasts on men's blood;
  Trenn shall be called a shining town.

Translated from the Welsh of an anonymous ninth century poet.

Idris Davies 1905 - 53

There's a concert in the village to buy us boots and bread

There's a concert in the village to buy us boots and bread,
There's a service in the chapel to make us meek and mild,
And in the valley town the draper's shop is shut.
The brown dogs snap at the stranger in silk,
And the winter ponies nose the buckets in the street.
The 'Miners' Arms' is quiet, the barman half afraid,
And the heroes of newspaper columns on explosion day
Are nearly tired of being proud.
But the widow on the hillside remembers a bitterer day,
The rap at the door and the corpse and the crowd,
And the parson's powerless words.
And her daughters are in London serving dinner to my lord,
And her single son, so quiet, broods on his luck in the queue.

Consider famous men, Dai bach, consider famous men

Consider famous men, Dai bach, consider famous men,
All their slogans, all their deeds,
And follow the funerals to the grave.
Consider the charlatans, the shepherds of the sheep!
Consider the grease upon the tongue, the hunger of the purse!
Consider the fury of the easy words,
The vulgarity behind the brass,
The dirty hands that shook the air, that stained the sky!

Yet some there were who lived for you,
Who lay to die remembering you.

Mabon was your champion once upon a time
And his portrait's on the milk-jug yet.
The world has bred no champions for a long time now,
Except the boxing, tennis, golf, and Fascist kind,
And the kind that democracy breeds and feeds for Harringay
And perhaps the world has grown too bitter or too wise
To breed a prophet or a poet ever again.

Mrs. Evans fach, you want butter again

Mrs. Evans fach, you want butter again.
How will you pay for it now, little woman
With your husband out on strike, and full
Of the fiery language? Ay, I know him,
His head is full of fire and brimstone
And a lot of palaver about communism,
And me, little Dan the Grocer
Depending so much on private enterprise.

What, depending on the miners and their
Money too? O yes, in a way, Mrs. Evans,
Yes, in a way I do, mind you.
Come tomorrow, little woman, and I'll tell you then
What I have decided overnight.
Go home now and tell that rash red husband of yours
That your grocer cannot afford to go on strike
Or what would happen to the butter from Carmarthen?
Good day for now, Mrs. Evans fach.

Send out your homing pigeons, Dai

Send out your homing pigeons, Dai,
Your blue-grey pigeons, hard as nails,
Send them with messages tied to their wings,
Words of your anger, words of your love.
Send them to Dover, to Glasgow, to Cork,
Send them to the wharves of Hull and of Belfast,
To the harbours of Liverpool and Dublin and Leith,
Send them to the islands and out of the oceans,
To the wild wet islands of the northern sea
Where little grey women go out in heavy shawls
At the hour of dusk to gaze on the merciless waters,
And send them to the decorated islands of the south
Where the mineowner and his tall stiff lady
Walk round and round the rose-pink hotel, day after day after day.
Send out your pigeons, Dai, send them out
With words of your anger and your love and your pride,
With stern little sentences wrought in your heart,
Send out your pigeons, flashing and dazzling towards the sun.

Go out, pigeons bach, and do what Dai tells you.

Let's go to Barry Island, Maggie fach

Let's go to Barry Island, Maggie fach,
And give all the kids one day by the sea,
And sherbet and buns and paper hats,
And a rattling ride on the Figure Eight;
We'll have tea on the sands, and rides on the donkeys,
And sit in the evening with the folk of Cwm Rhondda,
Singing the sweet old hymns of Pantycelyn
When the sun goes down beyond the rocky islands.
Come on, Maggie fach, or the train will be gone

Then the kids will be howling at home all day,
Sticky with dirt and gooseberry jam.
Leave the washing alone for today, Maggie fach,
And put on your best and come out to the sun
And down to the holiday sea.
We'll carry the sandwiches in a big brown bag
And leave our troubles behind for a day
With the chickens and the big black tips
And the rival soup-kitchens, quarrelling like hell.
Come, Maggie fach, with a rose on your breast
And an old Welsh tune on your little red lips,
And we'll all sing together in the Cardiff train
Down to the holiday sea.

Do you remember 1926?

Do you remember 1926? That summer of soups and speeches,
The sunlight on the idle wheels and the deserted crossings,
And the laughter and the cursing in the moonlit streets?
Do you remember 1926? The slogans and the penny concerts,
The jazz-bands and the moorland picnics,
And the slanderous tongues of famous cities?
Do you remember 1926? The great dream and the swift disaster
The fanatic and the traitor, and more than all,
The bravery of the simple, faithful folk?
'Ay, ay, we remember 1926,' said Dai and Shinkin,
As they stood on the kerb in Charing Cross Road,
'And we shall remember 1926 until our blood is dry.'

Tonypandy (extract)

The dusk deepens into the autumn night,
The cold drizzle spreads across the valleys,
The rubbish heaps are lost among the mists,
And where will you go for the evening, Dai,
For the evening in Tonypandy?
Will you count your coppers and join
The cinema queue where the tired women
Huddle like sheep, and comfort one another
With signs and sentimental phrases,
And where some folk blame the local councillors
For all the evils of the day and night?
O in the little queue, what tales are told
When we have shuffled off the burdens of the day –
What rancour, what compassion, what relief!
Or perhaps you will go to the prayer meeting down the chapel,
Where the newest member can pray for an hour without stopping,
The one converted at the last Big Meeting.
Or will you go to the pub at the corner
Where tongues come loose and hearts grow soft,
Where politics are so easy to understand,
Where the Irish labourer explains the constitution of de Valera,
And the Tory Working Man snarls behind his beer
At those who do not worship Winston Churchill,
And those who vaguely praise the Beveridge Report.
Or perhaps you will go back to your fireside this evening
And talk with your Martha of the children abroad,
The son out in Italy, the quick-tongued Ifor,
And the young quiet Emrys in the R.A.F.,
And Mair, with her roses and her laughing eyes,
So sprightly in her khaki uniform;
And you will be proud and you will be sad,
And you will be brave for Martha's sake,
And you will be Dai the great of heart.

Land of my mothers

Land of my mothers, how shall my brothers praise you?
With timbrels or rattles or tins?
With fire.
How shall we praise you on the banks of the rhymneying waters,
On the smoky shores and the glittering shores of Glamorgan,
On wet mornings in the bare fields behind the Newport docks,
On fine evenings when lovers walk by Bedwellty Church,
When the cuckoo calls to miners coming home to Rhymney Bridge,
When the wild rose defies the Industrial Revolution
And when the dear old drunken lady sings of Jesus and a little shilling.

Come down, O girls of song, to the bank of the coal canal
At twilight, at twilight
When mongrels fight
And long rats bite
Under the shadows of pit-head light,
And dance, you daughters of Gwenllian,
Dance in the dust in the lust of delight.

And you who have prayed in golden pastures
And oiled the wheels of the Western Tradition
And trod where bards have danced to church,
Pay a penny for this fragment of a burning torch.
It will never go out.

It will gather unto itself all the fires
That blaze between the heavens above and the earth beneath
Until the flame shall frighten each mud-hearted hypocrite
And scatter the beetles fattened on the cream of corruption,
The beetles that riddle the ramparts of Man.

Pay a penny for my singing torch,
O my sisters, my brothers of the land of my mothers,
The land of our fathers, our troubles, our dreams,
The land of Llewellyn and Shoni bach Shinkin,
The land of the sermons that pebble the streams,
The land of the englyn and Crawshay's old engine,
The land that is sometimes as proud as she seems.

And sons of the mountains and sons of the valleys
O lift up your hearts, and then
Lift up your feet.

Glyn Jones   b. 1905

The seagull

Gracing the tide-warmth, this seagull,
The snow-semblanced, moon-matcher,
The sun-shard and sea-gauntlet
Floating, the immaculate loveliness.
The feathered one, fishfed, the swift-proud,
Is buoyant, breasting the combers.
Sea-lily, fly to this anchor to me,
Perch your webs on my hand.
You nun among ripples, habited
Brilliant as paper-work, come.
Girl-glorified you shall be, pandered to,
Gaining that castle mass, for fortalice.
Scout them out, seagull, those glowing battlements,
Reconnoitre her, the Eigr-complexioned.
Repeat my pleas, my citations, go
Girlward, gull, where I ache to be chosen.
She solus, pluck up courage, accost her,
Stress your finesse to the fastidious one;
Use honeyed diplomacy, hinting
I cannot remain extant without her.
I worship her, every particle worships!
Look, friends, not old Merddin, hot-hearted,
Not Taliesin the bright-browed, beheld
The superior of this one in loveliness.
Cypress-shapely, but derisive beneath
Her tangled crop of copper, gull,
O, when you eye all Christendom's
Loveliest cheek—this girl will bring
Annihilation upon me, should your answer
Sound, gull, no relenting note.

Translated from the Welsh of Dafydd ap Gwilym (c. *1320–80*).

Esyllt

As he climbs down our hill, my kestrel rises,
Steering in silence up from five empty fields,
A smooth sun brushed brown across his shoulders,
Floating in wide circles, his warm wings stiff.
Their shadows cut; in new soft orange hunting boots
My lover crashes through the snapping bracken.

The still gorse-hissing hill burns, brags gold broom's
Outcropping quartz; each touched bush spills dew.
Strangely last moment's parting was never sad,
But unreal like my promised years; less felt
Than this intense and silver snail calligraphy
Scrawled here in the sun across these stones.

Why have I often wanted to cry out
More against his going when he has left my flesh
Only for the night? When he has gone out
Hot from my mother's kitchen, and my combs
Were on the table under the lamp, and the wind
Was banging the doors of the shed in the yard.

Merthyr

Lord, when they kill me, let the job be thorough
And carried out behind that county borough
Known as Merthyr, in Glamorganshire.
It would be best if it could happen, Sir,
Upon some great green roof, some Beacon slope
Those monstrous clouds of childhood slid their soap
Snouts over, into the valley. The season,
Sir, for shooting, summer; and love the reason.
On that hill, varnished in the glazing tide
Of evening, stand me, with the petrified

Plantations, the long blue spoonful of the lake,
The gold stook-tufted acres without break
Below me, and the distant corduroy
Glass of the river – which, a mitching boy,
I fished – flowing as though to quench
The smouldering coalfield in its open trench
Of steamy valley, fifteen miles away.
Here, Sir, are more arrangements for that day: –
Lay me, lead-loaded, below the mourning satin
Of some burnt-out oak; the skylark's chirpy Latin
Be my '*Daeth yr awr*'; gather the black
Flocks for bleaters – sweet grass their ham – upon the back
Of lonely Fan Gihirich; let night's branchy tree
Glow with silver-coated planets over me.

And yet, some times, I can't help wondering:
Is this rather posh poetic death the thing
After all, for somebody like me? I realize
I have a knack for telling bardic lies,
To say I see in some protean hill
A green roof, ship's prow or an eagle's bill,
To claim the mountain stream for me's as clear
As flowing gin, and yet as brown as beer.
I fancy words, some critics praise me for
A talent copious in metaphor.
But this my gift for logopoeic dance
Brothers, I know, a certain arrogance
Of spirit, a love of grandeur, style and dash,
Even vain-glory, the gaudiest *panache*,
Which might impel to great rascality
A heedless heart. This glorying in all
Created things, the golden sun, the small
Rain riding in the wind, the silvery shiver
Of the dawn-touched birches, and the chromium river,
Innocent itself, has yet calamitous
And wilful pride for child and famulus.
And thus I see the point when puritan
Or mystic poet harried under ban

Sensual nature, earth, sea and firmament;
I apprehend some strain of what they meant,
And look at nature with a wary eye.
Sir, that death I sought was pure effrontery.

Lord, when they kill me, let the job be thorough
And carried out *inside* that county borough
Known as Merthyr, in Glamorganshire,
A town easy enough to cast a slur
Upon, I grant. Some cyclopean ball
Or barn-dance, some gigantic free-for-all,
You'd guess, had caused her ruins, and those slums –
Frightening enough, I've heard, to daunt the bums –
Seem battered wreckage in some ghastly myth,
Some nightmare of the busting aerolith.
In short, were she a horse, so her attackers
Claim, her kindest destination were the knackers.
Yet, though I've been in Dublin, Paris, Brussels,
London, of course, too, I find what rustles
Oftenest and scentiest through the torpid trees
Of my brain-pan, is some Merthyr-mothered breeze,
Not dreams of them; a zephyr at its best
Acting on arrogance like the alkahest.

An object has significance or meaning
Only to the extent that human feeling
And intellect bestow them. All that sensational news
The heart hears, before she starts to bruise
Herself against the universe's rocky rind,
Is what she treasures most – the sight of wind
Fretting a great beech like an anchored breaker;
The vale, pink-roofed at sunset, a heavenly acre
Of tufted and irradiated toothpaste; the moon
Glistening sticky as snail-slime in the afternoon;
Street-papers hurdling, like some frantic foal,
The crystal barriers of squalls; the liquid coal
Of rivers; the hooter's loud liturgic boom;
Pit-clothes and rosin fragrant in a warm room –

Such sensations deck a ruinous scene
(To strangers) with tinsel, scarlet, spangles, green,
Gold, ribbons, and the glare of pantomime's
Brilliancy in full floods, foots and limes.

But far more than the scene, the legendary
Walkers and actors of it, the memory
Of neighbours, worthies, relatives,
Their free tripudiation, is what gives
That lump of coal that Shelley talks about
Oftenest a puff before it quite goes out.
My grandfather's fantastic friends, old Sion
O Ferthyr, occultist, meddler with the unknown –
(The spirits in malevolence one night
Nigh strangled him, but sobered Sion showed fight!)
My grandfather himself, musician, bard,
Pit-sinker, joker, whom the Paddys starred
As basser for their choir – so broken out!
My undersized great granny, that devout
Calvinist, with mind and tongue like knives;
The tall boys from Incline Top, and those boys' wives;
The tailor we believed a Mexican,
A rider of the prairies; Dr Pan
Jones (he it was who gave my father
The snowy barn-owl) Bishop – *soi-disant* rather;
Refined Miss Rees; Miss Thomas ditto; Evan
Davies, and the Williamses from Cefn.
Sir, where memories, dense as elephant
Grass, of these swarm round, in some common *pant*
Or hilltop lay me down; may the ghostly breeze
Of their presence be all my obsequies;
Not sheep and birds about me, but lively men,
And dead men's histories, O Lord. Amen.

Ambush

Midnight, and the new moon sunk.
Into the wood the soldier peers.
In dread and dark the forest seems
An army resting on its spears.

Oh, hostile spears, spare this boy,
In anguish now, before the fight,
Butchering fears who find his heart
Their forest and their moonless night.

He hears the crash, and sees the glare
On rocking trees and quaking land.
One dewdrop, in a gentle curve,
Falls, a soft jewel, upon his hand.

A new throb thunders through his heart;
He lies in stupor at this sign;
In death and dark the eternal pause
Is proffered now, like bread and wine.

And now, with ghostly eucharist,
He feels the heavenly hungers fed;
For him, on grave and heaving ground,
The auguries of love are spread.

Morning

On the night beach, quiet beside the blue
Bivouac of sea-wood, and fresh loaves, and the
Fish baking, the broken ghost, whose flesh burns
Blessing the dark bay and the still mast-light,
Shouts, 'Come'.
         A naked man on deck who heard
Also cockcrow, turning to the pebbles, sees
A dawn explode among the golden boats,
Pulls on his sea-plaid, leaps into the sea.

Wading the hoarfrost meadows of that fiord's
Daybreak, he, hungering fisherman, forgets
Cockcrow tears, dark noon, dead god, empty cave,
All the mountains of miraculous green
Light that swamped the landing punt, and kneels,
Shivering, in a soaked blouse, eating by the
Blue blaze the sweet breakfast of forgiveness.

Nain (extract from *The dream of Jake Hopkins*)

Do you remember the grandmother of those days?
Do you remember, when the whole sky was ablaze,
And the crimson sunball, evulsed and fiery, stood
Dissolving on the hillcrest? A heavy figure, broad
And black, floated out of that bonfire, as it were
Upon a rolling raft of warm illumination.
Slowly, encumbered and laborious,
She shepherded her shadow down the slope,
Her cloakful of vast flesh, with the ponderous budge
Of each slow, clog-clad foot, swaying against
The great out-dazzling hump of hilltop radiance.
Returning from her prayer-meeting, she, your Nain,
Wore her long black boat-cloak; on her head her black

Cloth hat darkened her swarthy features, alien,
Wrinkled like grain in wood, and the downbent
Cartwheel brim brushed the broad spreads and superstructures
Of her shoulders. She reached her garden rowan tree
And eyed with mildness, love and benediction all
The wide sweep of the mining valley. Then, turning back,
Looked at the cut sun and the afterglow, her guttered face
Lit up like a rock of clear crystal, her body,
Black and opaque, glowed warm, while momentary
Light and starlight inhabited her glistening skirts.
With shouts and singing limbs you reached her side,
She was your radiant Nain, your glossy one, whose harsh
Fingers were gentle as a harp-hand on your curls.

Vernon Watkins   1906 - 67

The heron

The cloud-backed heron will not move:
He stares into the stream.
He stands unfaltering while the gulls
And oyster-catchers scream.
He does not hear, he cannot see
The great white horses of the sea,
But fixes eyes on stillness
Below their flying team.

How long will he remain, how long
Have the grey woods been green?
The sky and the reflected sky,
Their glass he has not seen,
But silent as a speck of sand
Interpreting the sea and land,
His fall pulls down the fabric
Of all that windy scene.

Sailing with clouds and woods behind,
Pausing in leisured flight,
He stepped, alighting on a stone,
Dropped from the stars of night.
He stood there unconcerned with day,
Deaf to the tumult of the bay,
Watching a stone in water,
A fish's hidden light.

Sharp rocks drive back the breaking waves,
Confusing sea with air.
Bundles of spray blown mountain-high
Have left the shingle bare.
A shipwrecked anchor wedged by rocks,
Loosed by the thundering equinox,
Divides the herded waters,
The stallion and his mare.

Yet no distraction breaks the watch
Of that time-killing bird.
He stands unmoving on the stone;
Since dawn he has not stirred.
Calamity about him cries,
But he has fixed his golden eyes
On water's crooked tablet,
On light's reflected word.

Peace in the Welsh hills

Calm is the landscape when the storm has passed,
Brighter the fields, and fresh with fallen rain.
Where gales beat out new colour from the hills
Rivers fly faster, and upon their banks
Birds preen their wings, and irises revive.
Not so the cities burnt alive with fire
Of man's destruction: when their smoke is spent,
No phoenix rises from the ruined walls.

I ponder now the grief of many rooms.
Was it a dream, that age, when fingers found
A satisfaction sleeping in dumb stone,
When walls were built responding to the touch
In whose high gables, in the lengthening days,
Martins would nest? Though crops, though lives, would fail,
Though friends dispersed, unchanged the walls would stay,
And still those wings return to build in Spring.

Here, where the earth is green, where heaven is true
Opening the windows, touched with earliest dawn,
In the first frost of cool September days,
Chrysanthemum weather, presaging great birth,
Who in his heart could murmur or complain:
'The light we look for is not in this land?'
That light is present, and that distant time
Is always here, continually redeemed.

There is a city we must build with joy
Exactly where the fallen city sleeps.
There is one road through village, town and field,
On whose robust foundation Chaucer dreamed
A ride could wed the opposites in man.
There proud walls may endure, and low walls feed
The imagination if they have a vine
Or shadowy barn made rich with gathered corn.

Great mansions fear from their surrounding trees
The invasion of a wintry desolation
Filling their rooms with leaves. And cottages
Bring the sky down as flickering candles do,
Leaning on their own shadows. I have seen
Vases and polished brass reflect black windows
And draw the ceiling down to their vibrations,
Thick, deep, and white-washed, like a bank of snow.

To live entwined in pastoral loveliness
May rest the eyes, throw pictures on the mind,
But most we need a metaphor of stone
Such as those painters had whose mountain-cities
Cast long, low shadows on the Umbrian hills.
There, in some courtyard on the cobbled stone,
A fountain plays, and through a cherub's mouth
Ages are linked by water in the sunlight.

All of good faith that fountain may recall,
Woman, musician, boy, or else a scholar
Reading a Latin book. They seem distinct,
And yet are one, because tranquillity
Affirms the Judgment. So, in these Welsh hills,
I marvel, waking from a dream of stone,
That such a peace surrounds me, while the city
For which all long has never yet been built.

Great nights returning

Great nights returning, midnight's constellations
Gather from groundfrost that unnatural brilliance.
Night now transfigures, walking in the starred ways,
Tears for the living.

Earth now takes back the secret of her changes.
All the wood's dropped leaves listen to your footfall.
Night has no tears, no sound among the branches;
Stopped is the swift stream.

Spirits were joined when hazel leaves were falling.
Then the stream hurrying told of separation.
This is the fires' world, and the voice of Autumn
Stilled by the death-wand.

Under your heels the icy breath of Winter
Hardens all roots. The Leonids are flying.
Now the crisp stars, the circle of beginning;
Death, birth, united.

Nothing declines here. Energy is fire-born.
Twigs catch like stars or serve for your divining.
Lean down and hear the subterranean water
Crossed by the quick dead.

Now the soul knows the fire that first composed it
Sinks not with time but is renewed hereafter.
Death cannot steal the light which love has kindled
Nor the years change it.

Taliesin in Gower

Late I return, O violent, colossal, reverberant, eavesdropping sea.
My country is here. I am foal and violet. Hawthorn breaks from my hands.
I watch the inquisitive cormorant pry from the praying rock of Pwlldu,
Then skim to the gulls' white colony, to Oxwich's cockle-strewn sands.

I have seen the curlew's triangular print, I know every inch of his way.
I have gone through the door of the foundered ship, I have slept in the winch
    of the cave
With pine-log and unicorn-spiral shell secreting the colours of day;
I have been taught the script of the stones, and I know the tongue of the
    wave.

I witness here in a vision the landscape to which I was born,
Three smouldering bushes of willow, like trees of fire, and the course
Of the river under the stones of death, carrying the ear of corn
Withdrawn from the moon-dead chaos of rocks overlooking its secret force.

I see, a marvel in Winter's marshes, the iris break from its sheath
And the dripping branch in the ache of sunrise frost and shadow redeem
With wonder of patient, living leaf, while Winter, season of death,
Rebukes the sun, and grinds out men's groans in the voice of its underground
    stream.

Yet now my task is to weigh the rocks on the level wings of a bird,
To relate these undulations of time to a kestrel's motionless poise.
I speak, and the soft-running hour-glass answers; the core of the rock is a third:
Landscape survives, and these holy creatures proclaim their regenerate joys.

I know this mighty theatre, my footsole knows it for mine.
I am nearer the rising pewit's call than the shiver of her own wing.
I ascend in the loud waves' thunder, I am under the last of the nine.
In a hundred dramatic shapes I perish, in the last I live and sing.

All that I see with my sea-changed eyes is a vision too great for the brain.
The luminous country of auk and eagle rocks and shivers to earth.
In the hunter's quarry this landscape died; my vision restores it again.
These stones are prayers; every boulder is hung on a breath's miraculous birth.

Gorse breaks on the steep cliff-side, clings earth, in patches blackened for
    sheep,
For grazing fired; now the fair weather comes to the ravens' pinnacled knoll.
Larks break heaven from the thyme-breathing turf; far under, flying through
    sleep,
Their black fins cutting the rainbow surf, the porpoises follow the shoal.

They are gone where the river runs out, there where the breakers divide
The lacework of Three Cliffs Bay in a music of two seas;
A heron flaps where the sandbank holds a dyke to the twofold tide,
A wave-encircled isthmus of sound which the white bird-parliament flees.

Rhinoceros, bear and reindeer haunt the crawling glaciers of age
Beheld in the eye of the rock, where a javelin'd arm held stiff,
Withdrawn from the vision of flying colours, reveals, like script on a page,
The unpassing moment's arrested glory, a life locked fast in the cliff.

Now let the great rock turn. I am safe with an ear of corn,
A repository of light once plucked, from all men hidden away.
I have passed through a million changes. In a butterfly coracle borne,
My faith surmounting the Titan, I greet the prodigious bay.

I celebrate you, marvellous forms. But first I must cut the wood,
Exactly measure the strings, to make manifest what shall be.
All earth being weighed by an ear of corn, all heaven by a drop of blood.
How shall I loosen this music to the listening, eavesdropping sea?

Returning to Goleufryn

Returning to my grandfather's house, after this exile
From the coracle-river, long left with a coin to be good,
Returning with husks of those venturing ears for food
To lovely Carmarthen, I touch and remember the turnstile
Of this death-bound river. Fresh grass. Here I find that crown
In the shadow of dripping river-wood; then look up to the burning mile
Of windows. It is Goleufryn, the house on the hill;
And picking a child's path in a turn of the Towy I meet the prodigal town.

Sing, little house, clap hands: shut, like a book of the Psalms,
On the leaves and pressed flowers of a journey. All is sunny
In the garden behind you. The soil is alive with blind-petalled blooms
Plundered by bees. Gooseberries and currants are gay
With tranquil, unsettled light. Breathless light begging alms
Of the breathing grasses bent over the river of tombs
Flashes. A salmon has swallowed the tribute-money
Of the path. On the farther bank I see ragged urchins play

With thread and pin. O lead me that I may drown
In those earlier cobbles, reflected; a street that is strewn with palms,
Rustling with blouses and velvet. Yet I alone
By the light in the sunflower deepening, here stand, my eyes cast down
To the footprint of accusations, and hear the faint, leavening
Music of first Welsh words; that gust of plumes
'They shall mount up like eagles', dark-throated assumes,
Cold-sunned, low thunder and gentleness of the authentic Throne.

Yet now I am lost, lost in the water-wound looms
Where brief, square windows break on a garden's decay.
Gold butter is shining, the tablecloth speckled with crumbs.
The kettle throbs. In the calendar harvest is shown,
Standing in sheaves. Which way would I do you wrong?
Low, crumbling doorway of the infirm to the mansions of evening,
And poor, shrunken furrow where the potatoes are sown,
I shall not unnumber one soul I have stood with and known
To regain your stars struck by horses, your sons of God breaking in song.

Ode to Swansea

Bright town, tossed by waves of time to a hill,
Leaning Ark of the world, dense-windowed, perched
High on the slope of morning,
Taking fire from the kindling East:

Look where merchants, traders, and builders move
Through your streets, while above your chandlers' walls
Herring gulls wheel, and pigeons,
Mocking man and the wheelwright's art.

Prouder cities rise through the haze of time,
Yet, unenvious, all men have found is here.
Here is the loitering marvel
Feeding artists with all they know.

There, where sunlight catches a passing sail,
Stretch your shell-brittle sands where children play,
Shielded from hammering dockyards
Launching strange, equatorial ships.

Would they know you, could the returning ships
Find the pictured bay of the port they left
Changed by a murmuration,
Stained by ores in a nighthawk's wing?

Yes. Through changes your myth seems anchored here.
Staked in mud, the forsaken oyster beds
Loom; and the Mumbles lighthouse
Turns through gales like a seabird's egg.

Lundy sets the course of the painted ships.
Fishers dropping nets off the Gower coast
Watch them, where shag and cormorant
Perch like shades on the limestone rocks.

You I know, yet who from a different land
Truly finds the town of a native child
Nurtured under a rainbow,
Pitched at last on Mount Pleasant hill?

Stone-runged streets ascending to that crow's nest
Swinging East and West over Swansea Bay
Guard in their walls Cwmdonkin's
Gates of light for a bell to close.

Praise, but do not disturb, heaven's dreaming man
Not awakened yet from his sleep of wine.
Pray, while the starry midnight
Broods on Singleton's elms and swans.

The collier

When I was born on Amman hill
A dark bird crossed the sun.
Sharp on the floor the shadow fell;
I was the youngest son.

And when I went to the County School
I worked in a shaft of light.
In the wood of the desk I cut my name:
Dai for Dynamite.

The tall black hills my brothers stood;
Their lessons all were done.
From the door of the school when I ran out
They frowned to watch me run.

The slow grey bells they rung a chime
Surly with grief or age.
Clever or clumsy, lad or lout,
All would look for a wage.

I learnt the valley flowers' names
And the rough bark knew my knees.
I brought home trout from the river
And spotted eggs from the trees.

A coloured coat I was given to wear
Where the lights of the rough land shone.
Still jealous of my favour
The tall black hills looked on.

They dipped my coat in the blood of a kid
And they cast me down a pit,
And although I crossed with strangers
There was no way up from it.

Soon as I went from the County School
I worked in a shaft. Said Jim,
'You will get your chain of gold, my lad,
But not for a likely time.'

And one said, 'Jack was not raised up
When the wind blew out the light
Though he interpreted their dreams
And guessed their fears by night.'

And Tom, he shivered his leper's lamp
For the stain that round him grew;
And I heard mouths pray in the after-damp
When the picks would not break through.

They changed words there in darkness
And still through my head they run,
And white on my limbs is the linen sheet
And gold on my neck the sun.

Tom Earley b. 1911

Tiddlers

Here where the road now runs to Aberdare
the old canal lay stagnant in its bed
of reeds and rushes housing dragonflies
which flashed from sunshine into willow shade.

Beneath this very bridge we came to fish
for roach and perch and other smaller fry
like minnows, sticklebacks, and tiny frogs
and all these smelt peculiarly of pits.

A smell of stinkhorn-fungus, coal and damp
still clung to them as though they had swum up
some subterranean passage from the mine.

They smelt the house out when we got them home
and, when we changed the water, always died:
clean water killed them.

Rebel's progress

When idle in a poor Welsh mining valley,
Dissatisfied with two pounds five a week,
I got invited to a marxist rally
And found to my amazement I could speak.

I soon could spout about the proletariat,
The bourgeoisie and strikes and lockouts too,
Could run an AGM or commissariat
As well as boss-class secretaries do.

At first I joined Aneurin Bevan's party
But soon got disillusioned with all that.
Joined Harry Pollitt and became a commy.
They turned down all my pacifism flat.

The hungry thirties found me hunger marching
To squat with Hannington inside the Ritz.
Then PPU. For just this I'd been searching
Before the war and long before the blitz.

I liked the people in the Peace Pledge meeting
But found that they were holier than me
So marched with Collins and quite soon was greeting
My former comrades in the CND.

To sit with Russell next became my hobby,
Vanessa Redgrave's fame I hoped to share.
Got thrown around in Whitehall by a bobby
And then a broken arm in Grosvenor Square.

So now I'll leave the politics to others
And not be an outsider any more.
I'll go back to the valley, to my mother's,
And never set my foot outside the door.

Except to go to chapel on Bryn Sion
And maybe join the Cwmbach male voice choir,
I'll sit at home and watch the television
And talk about the rugby by the fire.

Brenda Chamberlain   b. 1912

To Dafydd Coed mourning his mountain-broken dog

Tears that you spill, clown David, crouched by rock
Have changed to nightmare quartzite, chips of granite.
The valley chokes with grief-stones wept from eyes
New-taught that death-scythes flash in the riven block
To reap warm entrails for a raven-harvest.
Withdrawn in stone-shot gully of the barren ground;
You mourn, baffled by crevice and goat height
Proving tricksy as dog-fox run to earth in the scree,
For one who lies in company of beetle-shard and sheep,
For him whose loose dropped brain and lungs hang coldly
Trembling from the flowered ledge down iceplant ways to silence.
The tears you shed are stone. So leave the dead to stand as monument.
Be shepherd friend again, clown grinning under wet eyes,
Stopping your ears to sound the valley breeds:
A corpse-man's cry for succour, a dead dog's howl.

Islandman

Full of years and seasoned like a salt timber
The island fisherman has come to terms with death.
His crabbed fingers are coldly afire with phosphorus
From the night-sea he fishes for bright-armoured herring.

Lifting his lobster pots at sunrise,
He is not surprised when drowned sailors
Wearing ropes of pearl round green throats,
Nod their heads at him from underwater forests.

His black-browed wife who sits at home
Before the red hearth, does not guess
That only a fishscale breastplate protects him
When he sets out across ranges of winter sea.

Song, Talysarn

Bone-aged is my white horse;
Blunted is the share;
Broken the man who through sad land
Broods on the plough.

Bone-bright was my gelding once;
Burnished was the blade;
Beautiful the youth who in green Spring
Broke earth with song.

R. S. Thomas   b. 1913

A peasant

Iago Prytherch his name, though, be it allowed,
Just an ordinary man of the bald Welsh hills,
Who pens a few sheep in a gap of cloud.
Docking mangels, chipping the green skin
From the yellow bones with a half-witted grin
Of satisfaction, or churning the crude earth
To a stiff sea of clods that glint in the wind –
So are his days spent, his spittled mirth
Rarer than the sun that cracks the cheeks
Of the gaunt sky perhaps once in a week.
And then at night see him fixed in his chair
Motionless, except when he leans to gob in the fire.
There is something frightening in the vacancy of his mind.
His clothes, sour with years of sweat
And animal contact, shock the refined,
But affected, sense with their stark naturalness.
Yet this is your prototype, who, season by season
Against siege of rain and the wind's attrition,
Preserves his stock, an impregnable fortress
Not to be stormed even in death's confusion.
Remember him, then, for he, too, is a winner of wars,
Enduring like a tree under the curious stars.

The Welsh hill country

Too far for you to see
The fluke and the foot-rot and the fat maggot
Gnawing the skin from the small bones,
The sheep are grazing at Bwlch-y-Fedwen,
Arranged romantically in the usual manner
On a bleak background of bald stone.

Too far for you to see
The moss and the mould on the cold chimneys,
The nettles growing through the cracked doors,
The houses stand empty at Nant-yr-Eira,
There are holes in the roofs that are thatched with sunlight,
And the fields are reverting to the bare moor.

Too far, too far to see
The set of his eyes and the slow phthisis
Wasting his frame under the ripped coat,
There's a man still farming at Ty'n-y-Fawnog,
Contributing grimly to the accepted pattern,
The embryo music dead in his throat.

Farm wife

Hers is the clean apron, good for fire
Or lamp to embroider, as we talk slowly
In the long kitchen, while the white dough
Turns to pastry in the great oven,
Sweetly and surely as hay making
In a June meadow; hers are the hands
Humble with milking, but still now
In her wide lap as though they heard
A quiet music, hers being the voice
That coaxes time back to the shadows
In the room's corners. O, hers is all
This strong body, the safe island
Where men may come, sons and lovers,
Daring the cold seas of her eyes.

Cynddylan on a tractor

Ah, you should see Cynddylan on a tractor.
Gone the old look that yoked him to the soil;
He's a new man now, part of the machine,
His nerves of metal and his blood oil.
The clutch curses, but the gears obey
His least bidding, and lo, he's away
Out of the farmyard, scattering hens.
Riding to work now as a great man should,
He is the knight at arms breaking the fields'
Mirror of silence, emptying the wood
Of foxes and squirrels and bright jays.
The sun comes over the tall trees
Kindling all the hedges, but not for him
Who runs his engine on a different fuel.
And all the birds are singing, bills wide in vain,
As Cynddylan passes proudly up the lane.

A Welsh testament

All right, I was Welsh. Does it matter?
I spoke the tongue that was passed on
To me in the place I happened to be,
A place huddled between grey walls
Of cloud for at least half the year.
My word for heaven was not yours.
The word for hell had a sharp edge
Put on it by the hand of the wind
Honing, honing with a shrill sound
Day and night. Nothing that Glyn Dŵr
Knew was armour against the rain's
Missiles. What was descent from him?

Even God had a Welsh name:
We spoke to him in the old language;
He was to have a peculiar care
For the Welsh people. History showed us
He was too big to be nailed to the wall
Of a stone chapel, yet still we crammed him
Between the boards of a black book.

Yet men sought us despite this.
My high cheek-bones, my length of skull
Drew them as to a rare portrait
By a dead master. I saw them stare
From their long cars, as I passed knee-deep
In ewes and wethers. I saw them stand
By the thorn hedges, watching me string
The far flocks on a shrill whistle.

And always there was their eyes' strong
Pressure on me: You are Welsh, they said;
Speak to us so; keep your fields free
Of the smell of petrol, the loud roar
Of hot tractors; we must have peace
And quietness.
              Is a museum
Peace? I asked. Am I the keeper
Of the heart's relics, blowing the dust
In my own eyes? I am a man;
I never wanted the drab role
Life assigned me, an actor playing
To the past's audience upon a stage
Of earth and stone; the absurd label
Of birth, of race hanging askew
About my shoulders. I was in prison
Until you came; your voice was a key
Turning in the enormous lock
Of hopelessness. Did the door open
To let me out or yourselves in?

Schoonermen

Great in this,
They made small ships do
Big things, leaping hurdles
Of the stiff sea, horse against horses
In the tide race.
              What has Rio
To do with Pwllheli? Ask winds
Bitter for ever
With their black shag. Ask the quays
Stained with spittle.
              Four days out

With bad cargo
Fever took the crew;
The mate and boatswain,
Peering in turn
Through the spray's window,
Brought her home. Memory aches
In the bones' rigging. If tales were tall,
Waves were taller.
                          From long years
In a salt school, caned by brine,
They came landward
With the eyes of boys,
The Welsh accent
Thick in their sails.

Those others

A gofid gwerin gyfan
Yn fy nghri fel taerni tân
                    Dewi Emrys

I have looked long at this land,
Trying to understand
My place in it – why,
With each fertile country
So free of its room,
This was the cramped womb
At last took me in
From the void of unbeing.

Hate takes a long time
To grow in, and mine
Has increased from birth;
Not for the brute earth
That is strong here and clean
And plain in its meaning
As none of the books are
That tell but of the war

Of heart with head, leaving
The wild birds to sing
The best songs; I find
This hate's for my own kind,
For men of the Welsh race
Who brood with dark face
Over their thin navel
To learn what to sell;

Yet not for them all either,
There are still those other
Castaways on a sea
Of grass, who call to me,
Clinging to their doomed farms;
Their hearts though rough are warm
And firm, and their slow wake
Through time bleeds for our sake.

Welsh history

We were a people taut for war; the hills
Were no harder, the thin grass
Clothed them more warmly than the coarse
Shirts our small bones.
We fought, and were always in retreat,
Like snow thawing upon the slopes
Of Mynydd Mawr; and yet the stranger
Never found our ultimate stand
In the thick woods, declaiming verse
To the sharp prompting of the harp.

Our kings died, or they were slain
By the old treachery at the ford.
Our bards perished, driven from the halls
Of nobles by the thorn and bramble.

We were a people bred on legends,
Warming our hands at the red past.
The great were ashamed of our loose rags
Clinging stubbornly to the proud tree
Of blood and birth, our lean bellies
And mud houses were a proof
Of our ineptitude for life.

We were a people wasting ourselves
In fruitless battles for our masters,
In lands to which we had no claim,
With men for whom we felt no hatred.

We were a people, and are so yet.
When we have finished quarrelling for crumbs
Under the table, or gnawing the bones
Of a dead culture, we will arise,
Armed, but not in the old way.

Lore

Job Davies, eighty-five
Winters old, and still alive
After the slow poison
And treachery of the seasons.

Miserable? Kick my arse!
It needs more than the rain's hearse,
Wind-drawn, to pull me off
The great perch of my laugh.

What's living but courage?
Paunch full of hot porridge,
Nerves strengthened with tea,
Peat-black, dawn found me

Mowing where the grass grew,
Bearded with golden dew.
Rhythm of the long scythe
Kept this tall frame lithe.

What to do? Stay green.
Never mind the machine,
Whose fuel is human souls.
Live large, man, and dream small.

Dylan Thomas 1914 - 53

The hunchback in the park

The hunchback in the park
A solitary mister
Propped between trees and water
From the opening of the garden lock
That lets the trees and water enter
Until the Sunday sombre bell at dark

Eating bread from a newspaper
Drinking water from the chained cup
That the children filled with gravel
In the fountain basin where I sailed my ship
Slept at night in a dog kennel
But nobody chained him up.

Like the park birds he came early
Like the water he sat down
And Mister they called Hey mister
The truant boys from the town
Running when he had heard them clearly
On out of sound

Past lake and rockery
Laughing when he shook his paper
Hunchbacked in mockery
Through the loud zoo of the willow groves
Dodging the park keeper
With his stick that picked up leaves.

And the old dog sleeper
Alone between nurses and swans
While the boys among willows
Made the tigers jump out of their eyes
To roar on the rockery stones
And the groves were blue with sailors

Made all day until bell time
A woman figure without fault
Straight as a young elm
Straight and tall from his crooked bones
That she might stand in the night
After the locks and chains

All night in the unmade park
After the railings and shrubberies
The birds the grass the trees the lake
And the wild boys innocent as strawberries
Had followed the hunchback
To his kennel in the dark.

A refusal to mourn the death, by fire, of a child in London

Never until the mankind making
Bird beast and flower
Fathering and all humbling darkness
Tells with silence the last light breaking
And the still hour
Is come of the sea tumbling in harness

And I must enter again the round
Zion of the water bead
And the synagogue of the ear of corn
Shall I let pray the shadow of a sound
Or sow my salt seed
In the least valley of sackcloth to mourn

The majesty and burning of the child's death.
I shall not murder
The mankind of her going with a grave truth
Nor blaspheme down the stations of the breath
With any further
Elegy of innocence and youth.

Deep with the first dead lies London's daughter,
Robed in the long friends,
The grains beyond age, the dark veins of her mother,
Secret by the unmourning water
Of the riding Thames.
After the first death, there is no other.

The force that through the green fuse drives the flower

The force that through the green fuse drives the flower
Drives my green age; that blasts the roots of trees
Is my destroyer.
And I am dumb to tell the crooked rose
My youth is bent by the same wintry fever.

The force that drives the water through the rocks
Drives my red blood; that dries the mouthing streams
Turns mine to wax.
And I am dumb to mouth unto my veins
How at the mountain spring the same mouth sucks.

The hand that whirls the water in the pool
Stirs the quicksand; that ropes the blowing wind
Hauls my shroud sail.
And I am dumb to tell the hanging man
How of my clay is made the hangman's lime.

The lips of time leech to the fountain head;
Love drips and gathers, but the fallen blood
Shall calm her sores.
And I am dumb to tell a weather's wind
How time has ticked a heaven round the stars.

And I am dumb to tell the lover's tomb
How at my sheet goes the same crooked worm.

Poem in October

It was my thirtieth year to heaven
Woke to my hearing from harbour and neighbour wood
    And the mussel pooled and the heron
        Priested shore
    The morning beckon
With water praying and call of seagull and rook
And the knock of sailing boats on the net webbed wall
        Myself to set foot
            That second
    In the still sleeping town and set forth.

My birthday began with the water-
Birds and the birds of the winged trees flying my name
   Above the farms and the white horses
       And I rose
      In rainy autumn
And walked abroad in a shower of all my days.
High tide and the heron dived when I took the road
      Over the border
       And the gates
Of the town closed as the town awoke.

   A springful of larks in a rolling
Cloud and the roadside bushes brimming with whistling
   Blackbirds and the sun of October
      Summery
     On the hill's shoulder,
Here were fond climates and sweet singers suddenly
Come in the morning where I wandered and listened
   To the rain wringing
      Wind blow cold
In the wood faraway under me.

   Pale rain over the dwindling harbour
And over the sea wet church the size of a snail
   With its horns through mist and the cattle
      Brown as owls
     But all the gardens
Of spring and summer were blooming in the tall tales
Beyond the border and under the lark full cloud.
     There could I marvel
      My birthday
Away but the weather turned around.

It turned away from the blithe country
And down the other air and the blue altered sky
Streamed again a wonder of summer
With apples
Pears and red currants
And I saw in the turning so clearly a child's
Forgotten mornings when he walked with his mother
Through the parables
Of sun light
And the legends of the green chapels

And the twice told fields of infancy
That his tears burned my cheeks and his heart moved in mine.
These were the woods the river and sea
Where a boy
In the listening
Summertime of the dead whispered the truth of his joy
To the trees and the stones and the fish in the tide.
And the mystery
Sang alive
Still in the water and singingbirds.

And there could I marvel my birthday
Away but the weather turned around. And the true
Joy of the long dead child sang burning
In the sun.
It was my thirtieth
Year to heaven stood there then in the summer noon
Though the town below lay leaved with October blood.
O may my heart's truth
Still be sung
On this high hill in a year's turning.

In my craft or sullen art

In my craft or sullen art
Exercised in the still night
When only the moon rages
And the lovers lie abed
With all their griefs in their arms,
I labour by singing light
Not for ambition or bread
Or the strut and trade of charms
On the ivory stages
But for the common wages
Of their most secret heart.

Not for the proud man apart
From the raging moon I write
On these spindrift pages
Nor for the towering dead
With their nightingales and psalms
But for the lovers, their arms
Round the griefs of the ages,
Who pay no praise or wages
Nor heed my craft or art.

Fern Hill

Now as I was young and easy under the apple boughs
About the lilting house and happy as the grass was green,
     The night above the dingle starry,
          Time let me hail and climb
     Golden in the heydays of his eyes,
And honoured among wagons I was prince of the apple towns
And once below a time I lordly had the trees and leaves
          Trail with daisies and barley
     Down the rivers of the windfall light.

And as I was green and carefree, famous among the barns
About the happy yard and singing as the farm was home,
     In the sun that is young once only,
          Time let me play and be
     Golden in the mercy of his means,
And green and golden I was huntsman and herdsman, the calves
Sang to my horn, the foxes on the hills barked clear and cold,
          And the sabbath rang slowly
     In the pebbles of the holy streams.

All the sun long it was running, it was lovely, the hay
Fields high as the house, the tunes from the chimneys, it was air
     And playing, lovely and watery
          And fire green as grass.
     And nightly under the simple stars
As I rode to sleep the owls were bearing the farm away,
All the moon long I heard, blessed among stables, the night-jars
          Flying with the ricks, and the horses
     Flashing into the dark.

And then to awake, and the farm, like a wanderer white
With the dew, come back, the cock on his shoulder: it was all
   Shining, it was Adam and maiden,
     The sky gathered again
   And the sun grew round that very day.
So it must have been after the birth of the simple light
In the first, spinning place, the spellbound horses walking warm
   Out of the whinnying green stable
     On to the fields of praise.

And honoured among foxes and pheasants by the gay house
Under the new made clouds and happy as the heart was long,
   In the sun born over and over,
     I ran my heedless ways,
   My wishes raced through the house high hay
And nothing I cared, at my sky blue trades, that time allows
In all his tuneful turning so few and such morning songs
   Before the children green and golden
     Follow him out of grace,

Nothing I cared, in the lamb white days, that time would take me
Up to the swallow thronged loft by the shadow of my hand,
   In the moon that is always rising,
     Nor that riding to sleep
   I should hear him fly with the high fields
And wake to the farm forever fled from the childless land.
Oh as I was young and easy in the mercy of his means,
     Time held me green and dying
   Though I sang in my chains like the sea.

Do not go gentle into that good night

Do not go gentle into that good night,
Old age should burn and rave at close of day;
Rage, rage against the dying of the light.

Though wise men at their end know dark is right,
Because their words had forked no lightning they
Do not go gentle into that good night.

Good men, the last wave by, crying how bright
Their frail deeds might have danced in a green bay,
Rage, rage against the dying of the light.

Wild men who caught and sang the sun in flight,
And learn, too late, they grieved it on its way,
Do not go gentle into that good night.

Grave men, near death, who see with blinding sight
Blind eyes could blaze like meteors and be gay,
Rage, rage against the dying of the light.

And you, my father, there on the sad height,
Curse, bless, me now with your fierce tears, I pray.
Do not go gentle into that good night.
Rage, rage against the dying of the light.

Alun Lewis   1915 - 44

The mountain over Aberdare

From this high quarried ledge I see
The place for which the Quakers once
Collected clothes, my fathers' home,
Our stubborn bankrupt village sprawled
In jaded dusk beneath its nameless hills;
The drab streets strung across the cwm,
Derelict workings, tips of slag
The gospellers and gamblers use
And children scrutting for the coal
That winter dole cannot purvey;
Allotments where the collier digs
While engines hack the coal within his brain;
Grey Hebron in a rigid cramp,
White cheap-jack cinema, the church
Stretched like a sow beside the stream;
And mourners in their Sunday best
Holding a tiny funeral, singing hymns
That drift insidious as the rain
Which rises from the steaming fields
And swathes about the skyline crags
Till all the upland gorse is drenched
And all the creaking mountain gates
Drip brittle tears of crystal peace;
And in a curtained parlour women hug
Huge grief, and anger against God.

But now the dusk, more charitable than Quakers,
Veils the cracked cottages with drifting may
And rubs the hard day off the slate.
The colliers squatting on the ashtip
Listen to one who holds them still with tales,
While that white frock that floats down the dark alley
Looks just like Christ; and in the lane
The clink of coins among the gamblers
Suggests the thirty pieces of silver.

I watch the clouded years
Rune the rough foreheads of these moody hills,
This wet evening, in a lost age.

Raiders' dawn

Softly the civilized
Centuries fall,
Paper on paper,
Peter on Paul.

And lovers waking
From the night –
Eternity's masters,
Slaves of Time –
Recognize only
The drifting white
Fall of small faces
In pits of lime.

Blue necklace left
On a charred chair
Tells that Beauty
Was startled there.

All day it has rained

All day it has rained, and we on the edge of the moors
Have sprawled in our bell-tents, moody and dull as boors,
Groundsheets and blankets spread on the muddy ground
And from the first grey wakening we have found
No refuge from the skirmishing fine rain
And the wind that made the canvas heave and flap
And the taut wet guy-ropes ravel out and snap.
All day the rain has glided, wave and mist and dream,
Drenching the gorse and heather, a gossamer stream
Too light to stir the acorns that suddenly
Snatched from their cups by the wild south-westerly
Pattered against the tent and our upturned dreaming faces.
And we stretched out, unbuttoning our braces,
Smoking a Woodbine, darning dirty socks,
Reading the Sunday papers – I saw a fox
And mentioned it in the note I scribbled home; –
And we talked of girls, and dropping bombs on Rome,
And thought of the quiet dead and the loud celebrities
Exhorting us to slaughter, and the herded refugees;
– Yet thought softly, morosely of them, and as indifferently
As of ourselves or those whom we
For years have loved, and will again
Tomorrow maybe love; but now it is the rain
Possesses us entirely, the twilight and the rain.

And I can remember nothing dearer or more to my heart
Than the children I watched in the woods on Saturday
Shaking down burning chestnuts for the schoolyard's merry play,
Or the shaggy patient dog who followed me
By Sheet and Steep and up the wooded scree
To the Shoulder o' Mutton where Edward Thomas brooded long
On death and beauty – till a bullet stopped his song.

Dawn on the east coast

From Orford Ness to Shingle Street
The grey disturbance spreads
Washing the icy seas on Deben Head.

Cock pheasants scratch the frozen fields,
Gulls lift thin horny legs and step
Fastidiously among the rusted mines.

The soldier leaning on the sandbagged wall
Hears in the combers' curling rush and crash
His single self-centred monotonous wish;

And time is a froth of such transparency
His drowning eyes see what they wish to see;
A girl laying his table with a white cloth.

The light assails him from a flank,
Two carbons touching in his brain
Crumple the cellophane lanterns of his dream.

And then the day, grown feminine and kind,
Stoops with the gulfing motion of the tide
And pours his ashes in a tiny urn.

From Orford Ness to Shingle Street
The grey disturbance lifts its head
And one by one, reluctantly,
The living come back slowly from the dead.

Sacco writes to his son

I did not want to die. I wanted you,
You and your sister Inez and your mother.
Reject this death, my Dante, seek out Life,
Yet not the death-in-life that most men live.
My body aches . . . I think I hear you weep.
You must not weep. Tears are a waste of strength.
Seven years your mother wept, not as your mother,
But as my wife. So make her more your mother.
Take her the ways I know she can escape
From the poor soulness that so wearies her.
Take her into the country every Sunday,
Ask her the name of such and such a plant,
Gather a basket each of herbs and flowers,
Ask her to find the robin where he nests,
She will be happy then. Tears do no damage
That spring from gladness, though they scald the throat.
Go patiently about it. Not too much
Just yet, Dante, good boy. You'll know.

And for yourself, remember in the play
Of happiness you must not act alone.
The joy is in the sharing of the feast.
Also be like a man in how you greet
The suffering that makes your young face thin.
Be not perturbed if you are called to fight.
Only a fool thinks life was made his way,
A fool or the daughter of a wealthy house.
Husband yourself, but never stale your mind
With prudence or with doubting. I could wish
You saw my body slipping from the chair
Tomorrow. You'd remember that, my son,
And would not weigh the cost of our struggle
Against the product as a poor wife does.
But I'll not break your sleep with such a nightmare.
You looked so happy when you lay asleep . . .

But I have neither strength nor room for all
These thoughts. One single thought's enough
To fill immensity. I drop my pen . . .

I hope this letter finds you in good health,
My son, my comrade. Will you give my love
To Inez and your mother and my friends.
Bartolo also sends his greetings to you.
I would have written better and more simple
Except my head spins like a dancing top
And my hand trembles . . . I am Oh, so weak . . .

The Mahratta Ghats

The valleys crack and burn, the exhausted plains
Sink their black teeth into the horny veins
Straggling the hills' red thighs, the bleating goats
– Dry bents and bitter thistles in their throats –
Thread the loose rocks by immemorial tracks.
Dark peasants drag the sun upon their backs.

High on the ghat the new turned soil is red,
The sun has ground it to the finest red,
It lies like gold within each horny hand.
Siva has spilt his seed upon this land.

Will she who burns and withers on the plain
Leave, ere too late, her scraggy herds of pain,
The cow-dung fire and the trembling beasts,
The little wicked gods, the grinning priests,
And climb, before a thousand years have fled,
High as the eagle to her mountain bed
Whose soil is fine as flour and blood-red?

But no! She cannot move. Each arid patch
Owns the lean folk who plough and scythe and thatch
Its grudging yield and scratch its stubborn stones.
The small gods suck the marrow from their bones.

Who is it climbs the summit of the road?
Only the beggar bumming his dark load.
Who was it cried to see the falling star?
Only the landless soldier lost in war.

And did a thousand years go by in vain?
And does another thousand start again?

The peasants

The dwarf barefooted, chanting
Behind the oxen by the lake,
Stepping lightly and lazily among the thorntrees
Dusky and dazed with sunlight, half awake;

The women breaking stones upon the highway,
Walking erect with burdens on their heads,
One body growing in another body,
Creation touching verminous straw beds.

Across scorched hills and trampled crops
The soldiers straggle by.
History staggers in their wake.
The peasants watch them die.

Roland Mathias   b. 1915

The flooded valley

My house is empty but for a pair of boots:
The reservoir slaps at the privet hedge and uncovers the roots
And afterwards pats them up with a slack good will:
The sheep that I market once are not again to sell.
I am no waterman, and who of the others will live
Here, feeling the ripple spreading, hearing the timbers grieve?
The house I was born in has not long to stand:
My pounds are slipping away and will not wait for the end.

I will pick up my boots and run round the shire
To raise an echo louder than my fear.
Listen, Caerfanell, who gave me a fish for my stone,
Listen, I am alone, alone.
And Grwyney, both your rivers are one in the end
And are loved. If I command
You to remember me, will you, will you,
Because I was once at noon by your painted church of Patricio?
You did not despise me once, Senni, or run so fast
From your lovers. And O I jumped over your waist
Before sunrise or the flower was warm on the gorse.
You would do well to listen, Senni. There is money in my purse.

So you are quiet, all of you, and your current set away
Cautiously from the chapel ground in which my people lie . . .
Am I not Kedward, Prosser, Morgan, whose long stones
Name me despairingly and set me chains?
If I must quarrel and scuff in the weeds of another shire
When my pounds are gone, swear to me now in my weakness, swear
To me poor you will plant a stone more in this tightening field
And name there your latest dead, alas your unweaned feeblest child.

Remember Charlie Stones, carpenter

The stream is sultry and a short haze mulls it,
I in the hooved earth merry as a stick
Half-peeled and giving the horse-turds ample berth.
Here, having eaten, what in hysteria can I do
But wait, as shell and paper wait, myself
The best time to be thrown away? In every site
There is some aptitude, some haunched-up niche
Or bee-hide where the sourest litter
May so be decorous and quicker rotten.
Here close at hand too is the fear in which we are all begotten:
'Remember Charlie Stones, carpenter.'

Were your proportions, Charlie, seen as well
In time as in the Gill
Lettering widening your white stone under the seven trees?
Or did this bowl
Of hills burn like an August offering to the Lord
So that your soul cursed it
Three times with force and was afraid,
Prating as ill as I? Over this valley is a well
Beating with water and I do not see it,
The hills are shaped every day afresh with a new hand
And I do not feel it,
Only the sultry dancer under the seven trees
I know and the body's stirs
As it frets to change its ground.
Are you bound there, Charlie? By one or many?
Rattle the church-box louder and detect my penny.
I know too well to remember, Charlie Stones, carpenter.

A letter

Eight years ago come Tuesday now I walked
Big as a brown wind angry from your door.
Mad you had made me, Ellen Skone, talked
My tongue out of duty, crossed me more
That day than I remember. And the sun came down
Like a bakestone. Well, that was it! –
The widow lost her lodger in a fit
Of temper and the whole cliff laboured under frown.
I am no more a scrallion than I was,
Brawned out a bit as a haulier over Roose
As a matter of fact, and my close
Friends do tell me – God who has
Caught me enough in a lie prevent me now,
O now when I want the truth! Friends?
I have none. None that I trust like the hands
Of the clock on midnight and the slow
Matching of your rounded arms.
I am no fool to harp upon your charms
Like a twenty-oner, lose my pen in words
I can hardly spell. But listen, if it affords
You pleasure. I'm sorry. *Sorry.* Now
Answer me fairly, Ellen. This is my only throw.
Must you pretend like a Sunday child from home,
Play 'tisty-tosty, how long shall I live?'
The hay is carried and the high tides are come.
God in heaven, do only young men wive?

Craswall

With a long stirrup under fern
From a small blast of oaks and thorn
The shepherd scours the circling hill
And the sharp dingle creeping to the well.

A trickle from the canting neck
A pony coughing in the track
Are all the stranger hears, and steep
Among the fern the threading of the sheep.

This is the boundary: different burrs
Stick, stones make darker scars
On the road down: nightingales
Struggle with thorn-trees for the gate of Wales.

Departure in middle age

The hedges are dazed as cock-crow, heaps of leaves
Brushed back to them like a child's hair
After a sweat, and clouds as recently bundled
Out of the hollows whimper a little in the conifers higher up.
I am the one without tears, cold
And strange to myself as a stepfather encountered
For the first time in the passage from the front door.

But I cannot go back, plump up the pillow and shape
My sickness like courage. I have spent the night in a shiver:
Usk water passing now was a chatter under the Fan
When the first cold came on. They are all dead, all,
Or scattered, father, mother, my pinafore friends,
And the playground's echoes have not waited for my return.
Exile is the parcel I carry, and you know this,
Clouds, when you drop your pretences and the hills clear.

Cyril Hodges   b. 1915

The mead song of Taliesin

I have distilled the wisdom of industrious bees
Who stole the pollened summer, that the horn
Might brim bubbles of gold for winter ecstasies,
And we thus bear what else could not be borne.
Drinking the death of flowers, warmed by the death of trees,
All memories are soothed into a sleep
Grey and undreaming, while the folding centuries
Cover and hold what else we could not keep.

If my most pondered symbols waver and grow dim
And wander lost over the sin of time,
Say I was drunk and tired, and pay no heed to him
Parsing by babel in a maze of rhyme.
Say that an old man, senile, mumbling in his mead,
An older story rambling in his head,
Dribbled his druid nonsense and discerned no need
For further progress and, praise God, is dead.

And should the troubling vision break into this day
To set the sober mind of man afire,
Let not my archaic meaning shake the soul astray
From its ordained and self-excreted mire;
For my great olden book has known it all, and told
How like to like shall cleave. Our memories
Die as the sweetness melted into bubbling gold
When I distilled the wisdom of the bees.

Keidrych Rhys   b. 1915

The prodigal speaks

Yes born on Boxing Day among childlike virgin hills
Too isolated for foxhounds even explaining much more than horoscope hours
Far north of a fox-earth county never seen through rose-tinted glasses
Middle of war; hamlet called Bethlehem; one shop; chapel.

Almost a second Christ! say; only son of a tenant-
Farmer of hundred odd acres growing corn for red soldiers
Merrily with a daft boy from an industrial school who
Spoke in strange tongue across our great Silurian arc of sky.

Cloudroll over flying brontesque heights; this early photo
Fiery enough this rusty pocket-knife recall now
A two-mile walk to school alone along a Roman road
Geese-fright on common the little sempstress staying a fortnight.

Wheels scotched below the varnished meadowlands
A jack-in-the-box handed down from a badly-
Loaded trap back from market town steaming pony
Gentle to touch mad dual-purpose bull in lane near thing

Lost to parents for days every summer on black mountain
With endless views once faint after first experience moral
Deadly nightshade plovers eggs wind cool as air
Under dairy slabs the tallest tree in whole Carmarthenshire

Where hedging match meant more than holiday by sea
Stitches at sports then poaching salmon Ben Christmas
Dan Joshua the bastards how hold gun snipe otter – bobs
Are symbols to a returning self like mushrooms-in-dew oh balm!

Country folk all goggle-eyed outside a wedding inn
Damp dusks scarecrows whirring in a flickering light
Those secret see-saw spots that were our very own young hearts
Before deep crises and Eirlys dead puritans gipsies of yesterday good-bye!

Youth

I try to remember the things
At home that mean Wales but typical
Isn't translated across
The Channel: I try to create,
Doors grow into masts, love losses
In the village wood, but boyhood's
Fear fled into the pale skeleton
Of the dark mountain, into
The bilingual valley filled
Through a sail-hole of my drying
Feelings. But I try. Lightning
Is different in Wales.

Interlude

Simply I would sing for the time being
Of the wayward hills I must make my feeling.
The rickety bicycle, the language of birds
Caught fishing up the church street for preaching words,
The deacon hawking swedes, the gyppos clapping on
Their way to vans over common's crushed sandstone
And the milk stands so handy to sit upon!
The roadmen laying pipes of local cement
The Italian's chip shop and the village comment;
'No reserve, all they know on the tip of their tongue.'
That educated tramp from the lodging-house league.

The lady, the lake, both sleeping, the cattle
Called back through stories, bells silent, a deep down rattle:
Comics, rivers well-named, dense gorse floodlights valley's
Gurgling. Grief in a mailbag; drama on trolleys.
Less and less shoeing for smith, farming's polite dying,
"Messiah" in the chapel – but a warning, gulls crying
Up at Easter miners off the race's soothing colour.
Oh simply simply I sing down the masterly contour.

During lambing season

Side by side let elder sheep roll over on spring earth
huts are dry and full in Talley, china blue eyes write signs of birth.
Here's work for boys in long corduroys from Mothvey to Goldengrove
all through that summer's rogue Ryland ram's brief nonconformist love!
Oh the young devils are tough with bleeding navels lean on ground;
by elements torn, brown hairstuff licked, prayer suck, born worth a £.
Wander off like postman, sex by chapel ballot to save funeral expense
Still no need to ridicule Sabbath morning pack out of existence.
Up on a ditch one inhales fag's smoke on account of hand closed flesh,
their ears are made of a god's carpet, cut out; a penknife mesh;
too weak you say, well kitchen fire, whisky in a silver spoon, ma's ah!
false baba sentiment! these parents wear no bells; but the same happens baa
   baa;
low-bellied, hedge-breakers, man's bloody marvel, organized on purple hill:
do it with an arm in a sling; drown to a rook's rainy stare; die of woolball.

Soldiers in Scapa

I watch the plovers wheel low at dusk
Over the sparse-sown grass
Where soldiers trample with lobster-pot cricket bat
Into the wet canteen for a last drink.

Out of the blue of this 'sunny' island
Landlocked our padre walks, and chats
Of the native pleasures enjoyed in this land.

The islanders somewhat narrow, farmers,
Less interesting than the sailormen Shetlanders
How they eke out an existence God alone knows

Duststorms sand up all skyline visionary

Guillemots fishing-flighting across the narrows
Suffer more from boredom than silenced I;
Bird-winged – a floating island of despair, sure – the bay
A dark mind conditioned under Northern Lights.

O will millions know troopships destroyer escorts again
Ploughing past the roughed greenlands like explorer's boats?

Except in the great white motion of natural elementary flight
These tireless sea-geese rockwards go, so far
Defenceless – like a Harrovian brigadier's map-mind.

Tragic guilt

No. I'm not an Englishman with a partisan religion.
My roots lie in another region,
Though ranged alongside yours.

But I can sense your stubborness and your cohesion
And can even feel pride in your recent decisions
That anger reassures.

I know no love for disembodied principles, improbable tales.
The strength of the common man was always the strength of Wales,
Unashamed of her race.

May this be also England's role to bring to birth.
May she draw opposite new powers from the earth.
Huge Shakespeare has his place.

I have felt in my bones comradeship and pity,
I have seen wonders in an open door blitz city.

Amid tremendous history, new pity.

Lynette Roberts b. 1916

Poem from Llanybri

If you come my way that is . . .
Between now and then, I will offer you
A fist full of rock cress fresh from the bank
The valley tips of garlic red with dew
Cooler than shallots, a breath you can swank

In the village when you come. At noon-day
I will offer you a choice bowl of cawl
Served with a lover's spoon and a chopped spray
Of leeks or savori fach, not used now

In the old way you'll understand. The din
Of children singing through the eyelet sheds
Ringing 'smith hoops, chasing the butt of hens;
Or I can offer you Cwmcelyn spread

With quartz stones, from the wild scratchings of men;
You will have to go carefully with clogs
Or thick shoes for it's treacherous the fen,
The East and West Marshes also have bogs.

Then I'll do the lights, fill the lamp with oil,
Get coal from the shed, water from the well;
Pluck and draw pigeon with crop of green foil
This your good supper from the lime-tree fell.

A sit by the hearth with blue flames rising,
No talk. Just a stare at 'Time' gathering
Healed thoughts, pool insight, like swan sailing
Peace and sound around the home, offering

You a night's rest and my day's energy.
You must come, start this pilgrimage,
Can you come? – send an ode or elegy
In the old way and rise our heritage.

Nigel Heseltine   b. 1916

Denbigh Eisteddfod, 1939

An old man speaking of poetry
gave us no crown no chair
no father no mother no voice
for to-morrow

for to-morrow death for to-morrow
death (nobody's seen it easy, to say
death); for to-morrow (if we're sober)
maybe a crown.

The crowd wilted and muttered, the old man
cleared his right hand of the air,
his white hair in disgrace
cleared from the stage

speaking to poets in danger, 1,200 poets
hooted and hissed when that old man
gave them no crowns.

Hero of his village

Though you are missing from the shelf
where your family coffins rot in the vault,
your cross is on the church wall
decorated with a button or two from your coat.

So the children coming with the hymn-
books in their hands see that you died
for liberty or some cause and hang
above where the parish magazine is displayed.

Though there is nothing of you but the buttons,
those in the cricket-team you taught to bowl
remember you; the girls you looked aside from
lest you become entangled, married now
look beyond their solid husbands, remember you well.

Though you left no child, nor a wife
nor ploughed land save once on leave
as relaxation; though the parson leaving
his church in a hurry now never sees
your cross, yet given a proper occasion the man
could preach a sermon on your dying that would make
futile in comparison the longest life.

Harri Webb   b. 1920

Big night

We started drinking at seven
And went out for a breather at ten,
And all the stars in heaven
Said, 'Go back and drink again.'

Orion was furiously winking
As he gave us the green light
So we went back in to our drinking
Through the breakneck Brecknock night.

We were singers, strongmen and sages,
We were witty and wise and brave,
And all the ghosts of the ages
Applauded from Crawshay's grave.

The tipsy Taff was bawling
A non-traditional tune
And the owls of Pontsarn were calling
Rude names at the frosty moon,

And homeward we were staggering
As the Pandy clock struck three
And the stars of the Plough went swaggering
From Vaynor to Pengarnddu.

Old Glyn

Old Glyn, our milkman, came from down the country
Between Waunarlwydd and Mynydd Bach y Glo,
A neighbour of innumerable uncles and cousins
In an untidy region of marsh and pastures and mines.
He spoke Welsh of course, but was frequently too drunk
To talk in any language. His milk, though, was good
And his measure generous, as he splashed it into the jug
From a bright battered can with a big extra splash
For a good boy. The spokes of his light trap
And the big brass churn amidships shone in the sun
And his brisk mare Shan was a champion trotter;
And when I took the reins of a Saturday morning
(With Glyn's big paw still on them, just in case)
I drove the chariot of the sun, I was Caesar, Ben Hur,
I was a big boy, helping the milkman.
My parents said among themselves it was drink,
When Glyn stopped coming. I think it was the bottles
And the new ways, the zombie electric trolley,
The precisely measured pints. Nobody is cheated now,
There is nothing extra, splashed out in goodwill
For a good boy. I buy my milk in a tin.
It is a dry powder. They have ground Glyn's bones.

Thanks in winter

The day that Eliot died, I stood
By Dafydd's grave in Ystrad Fflur.
It was the depth of winter,
A day for an old man to die.
The dark memorial stone,
Chiselled in marble of Latin
And the soft intricate gold
Of the old language,
Echoed the weather's colour
A slate vault over Ffair Rhos,
Pontrhydfendigaid, Pumlumon,
The sheep runs, the rough pasture
And the lonely whitewashed houses
Scattered like frost, the dwellings
Of country poets, last inheritors
To the prince of song who lies
Among princes, among ruins.
A pilgrim under the yew at Ystrad Fflur
I kept my vow, prayed for my country,
Cursed England, came away
And home to the gas fire and television
News. Caught between two languages,
Both dying, I thanked the long-dead
Minstrel of May and the newly silent
Voice of the bad weather, the precise
Accent of our own time, taught
To the disinherited, offering
Iron for gold.

The stone face

Tywysog Aberffraw, hawddamor!
Arglwydd Eryri, henffych well!

It may of course be John his father-in-law,
Their worst, our best not easily distinguishable
After so many buried centuries. The experts
Cannot be sure, that is why they are experts.
But this stone face under a broken crown
Is not an impersonal mask of sovereignty;
This is the portrait of a living man
And when his grandson burnt Deganwy down
So that no foreign army should hold its strength,
I think they buried the head of Llywelyn Fawr
As primitive magic and for reasons of state.

No fortress was ever destroyed so utterly
As was Deganwy by Llywelyn the Last;
The thoroughness of despair, foreknown defeat,
Was in the burning and breaking of its walls.
But at some door or window a hand paused,
A raised crowbar halted by the stare
Of a stone face. The Prince is summoned
And the order given: Bury it in the earth,
There will be other battles, we'll be back –
Spoken in the special Welsh tone of voice
Half banter, half blind fervour, the last look
Exchanged between the hunted living eyes
And dead majesty for whom there are no problems.

The burning of Deganwy, the throne and fortress
Of Llywelyn Fawr shattered, his principality
Gone in the black smoke drifting over Menai
And his last heir forced into endless retreat
To the banks of Irfon and the final lance-thrust.
There was no return, no reverent unearthing.

A stone face sleeps beneath the earth
With open eyes. All history is its dream.
The Great Orme shepherds the changing weather,
On Menai's shores the tides and generations
Ebb, grumble and flow; harps and hymns sound
And fall silent; briefly the dream flares out of the eyes,
Then darkness comes again.

Seven hundred and fifty years of darkness.
Now, in a cold and stormy spring, we stand
At the unearthing of the sovereign head,
The human face under the chipped crown.
Belatedly, but not too late, the rendezvous is made.
The dream and the inheritors of the dream,
The founder and father, and those who must rebuild
The broken fortresses, re-establish the throne
Of eagles, here exchange the gaze of eagles
In the time of the cleansing of the eyes.

John Stuart Williams   b. 1920

Another island in the sun

Among the pines the cicadas weave
an undergrowth of sound; the muffled
sea drums on the off-beat and wood rubs
against stone as the boats acknowledge
their moorings to the ritual
rise and fall of tide. The sun sings like
a guitar struck with an open hand,
but here on this tawny beach, there is
no lucid counterpoint of bird-song.

Six miles away, across the dry fields,
a walled garden, riotous with flowers,
cool with the sound of rushing leaf, green
with the fall of fresh fountains, cheats the
searing sun, and in frail colonnades
of branch and vine the small birds squabble
and sing, the air alive with their light
and joyous copulation.
                              On this
island only a senor of much
capital can easily afford
the consolations of flight and song.

Theseus on Scyros

At Scyros, waiting for an end,
the lost days sing within his skull
like the half-forgotten music
of a distant feast, a confused
brightness clouded by the broken
fall of intervening seasons,
brave sounds, but incoherent now.
He lifts his face, its skin worn thin
as a dry leaf, towards the blaze
of brittle surf; behind blank eyes,
the lion gates of Mycenae,
the gilded dancers of the maze
and the catechizing horns whose
answers lie forgotten in the
sand with the blind and battered mask
of once implacable Minos.
That cypress on its folded hill
reminds him briefly of a black
sail from Crete, and Ariadne,
who taught him something of the strange
and random kindness of the heart
when the sea burned like a bronze harp.
Here on this cliff, where all comes to
a stop before the abrupt drop
of time, and the frail clouds feather
their fingers after lost desires,
he looks down at the rocks crouched like
bulls in the iridescent surf.
What he was, what had happened, came
in the end to one name, one place.

He turns to greet Lycomedes
without reproach, feels the thrust of
friendship, and sees with no surprise,
indeed with a sense of fitness,
the black bull rising from the sea.

Skokholm

At dusk great rafts of shearwaters
Rise and fall with the slow tide
And the island's edge and colour
Lose definition. The wide
Fingered buzzard spirals down.
No wind sucks the sun-dried
Grass: the air contracts, still, but alive . . .

Suddenly the mist explodes, the sense
Is bruised by buffeting wings, the night
Is luminous with noise as bird after bird
Comes swinging home. I light
My torch, and catch one spread on the turf
Before its gull-proof hole. It hooks its wings
And slides below, leaving flecks of surf
To trace its track on the yellow grass.

In the iridescent morning air
Below the singing bird-shot sky,
Their sharp wings spread like arms,
The lost shearwaters lie
Eviscerated by the gulls.
Those without deep-shelters die.

Images

After the long drag up from town,
Familiar tracks thick with bracken, snared
With bramble looped between stubby oaks,
Rest in this clearing, lie enferned and watch,
Spreadeagled, broken branch and crossed iron
Grid the high sun, the moving sky.

Here in this wood coigned on its shouldered hill,
Where the muted metal of shunted trucks below,
Softly percussive, filters through the trees
To point the pigeons' rough and lazy call,
The slow reverberation of shuffled light
Clouds the sense and blurs the edge of time.

The hard earth shifts beneath your back
And lost voices whisper in the spidered grass.
Your feeling fingers grope among dry roots
To grasp the broken breast-bone of a bird.

What faces hide behind these stony masks,
Thrusting their snouts between barred shadows?
What jagged figures gesture from these walls
Of black leaf and light? A thick finger of smoke
Insults the air. The slow trucks click
Behind a screen of trees, Dachau, Maidanek . . .

After the long drag up the narrow road
The helmed past lifts its visor when you least expect
And you lie pinned by images gone and to come.
Learn to know them; you brought them with you to this secret
Place and, like it or not, you'll take them away.

Overkill

Now gooth sunne under wode:
Me reweth, Marye, thy faire rode.
Now gooth sunne under tree:
Me reweth, Marye, thy sone and thee.

A funelled rage of fire and dust:
Me reweth, Marye, thy lost trust.
A whirlpool coiled in flesh and bone:
Me reweth, Marye, thee and thy sone.

The ravelled fibres of the cross:
Me reweth, Marye, thee and thy loss.
The signet fish burnt from the sand:
Me reweth, Marye, the broken bond.

The tree is split and fused in flame:
Me reweth, Marye, thy fair name.
The sun drags a barren stone:
Me reweth, Marye, thee and thy sone.

T. H. Jones 1921-65

Back?

Back is the question
Carried to me on the curlew's wing,
And the strong sides of the salmon.

Should I go back then
To the narrow path, the sheep turds,
And the birded language?

Back to an old, thin bitch
Fawning on my spit, writhing
Her lank belly with memories:

Back to the chapel, and a charade
Of the word of God made by a preacher
Without a tongue:

Back to the ingrowing quarrels,
The family where you have to remember
Who is not speaking to whom:

Back to the shamed memories of Glyn Dŵr
And Saunders Lewis's aerodrome
And a match at Swansea?

Of course I'd go back if somebody'd pay me
To live in my own country
Like a bloody Englishman.

But for now, lacking the money,
I must be content with the curlew's cry
And the salmon's taut belly

And the waves, of water and of fern
And words, that beat unendingly
On the rocks of my mind's country.

Rhiannon

My daughter of the Mabinogion name
Tells me Ayer's Rock is ten times higher than
A house, and she, being seven today,
Would like to see it, especially
To ride there on a camel from Alice Springs.
She also says she wants to be a poet –
Would the vision of that monolith
Stay in her mind and dominate her dreams
As in my mind and dreams these thirty years
There stays the small hill, Alltyclych,
The hill of bells, bedraggled with wet fern
And stained with sheep, and holding like a threat
The wild religion and the ancient tongue,
All the defeated centuries of Wales?

Difference

Under God's violent unsleeping eye
My fathers laboured for three hundred years
On the same farm, in the expected legend.
Their hymns were anodynes against defeat,
But sin, the original and withering worm,
Was always with them, whether they excelled
In prayers, made songs on winter nights,
Or slobbered in temptation, women, drink.

I inherit their long arms and mountain face,
The withering worm sleeps too within my blood
But I know loneliness, unwatched by God.

Welsh childhood

Eating the bread of the world
In the thin rain of time
The child ignores the crow,
The stoat, and worm who know
What bread and child will come
To, crumble to at last.

In comfort on harsh rock
Or lacerated pine,
Never out of the wind
Or the thin nails of rain,
He thinks that wind the breath
Of the world he knows is truth.

A bible in his mind,
A pulpit for his mouth,
Should he seek further for
The absence of the wind
Or accommodating truth,
Life's wound without a scar?

The crow, the stoat, the worm
Wait because they know
He will never be out of the wind,
As long as he has breath,
That breath is the truth
He crumbles to in the end.

Land of my fathers

Some frosty farmers fathered me to fare
Where their dreams never led, the sunned and blue
Salt acres where Menelaus once made ado
Because Paris also thought Helen was fair;
And now this ancient sunburnt country where
Everything's impossibly bright and new
Except what happens between me and you
When I ransack your bright and ravished hair.

Always I feel the cold and cutting blast
Of winds that blow about my native hills,
And know that I can never be content
In this or any other continent
Until with my frosty fathers I am at last
Back in the old country that sings and kills.

Leslie Norris   b. 1921

Water

On hot summer mornings my aunt set glasses
On a low wall outside the farmhouse,
With some jugs of cool water.
I would sit in the dark hall, or
    Behind the dairy window,
Waiting for children to come from the town.

They came in small groups, serious, steady,
And I could see them, black in the heat,
Long before they turned in at our gate
To march up the soft, dirt road.
    They would stand by the wall,
Drinking water with an engrossed thirst. The dog

Did not bother them, knowing them responsible
Travellers. They held in quiet hands their bags
Of jam sandwiches, and bottles of yellow fizz.
Sometimes they waved a gratitude to the house,
    But they never looked at us.
Their eyes were full of the mountain, lifting

Their measuring faces above our long hedge.
When they had gone I would climb the wall,
Looking for them among the thin sheep-runs.
Their heads were a resolute darkness among ferns,
    They climbed with unsteady certainty.
I wondered what it was they knew the mountain had.

They would pass the last house, Lambert's, where
A violent gander, too old by many a Christmas,
Blared evil warning from his bitten moor,
Then it was open world, too high and clear
        For clouds even, where over heather
The free hare cleanly ran, and the summer sheep.

I knew this; and I knew all summer long
Those visionary gangs passed through our lanes,
Coming down at evening, their arms full
Of cowslips, moondaisies, whinberries, nuts,
        All fruits of the sliding seasons,
And the enormous experience of the mountain

That I who loved it did not understand.
In the summer, dust filled our winter ruts
With a level softness, and children walked
At evening through golden curtains scuffed
        From the road by their trailing feet.
They would drink tiredly at our wall, talking

Softly, leaning, their sleepy faces warm for home.
We would see them murmur slowly through our stiff
Gate, their shy heads gilded by the last sun.
One by one we would gather up the used jugs,
        The glasses. We would pour away
A little water. It would lie on the thick dust, gleaming.

The ballad of Billy Rose

Outside Bristol Rovers' Football Ground –
The date has gone from me, but not the day,
Nor how the dissenting flags in stiff array
Struck bravely out against the sky's grey round –

Near the Car Park then, past Austin and Ford,
Lagonda, Bentley, and a colourful patch
Of country coaches come in for the match
Was where I walked, having travelled the road

From Fishponds to watch Portsmouth in the Cup.
The Third Round, I believe. And I was filled
With the old excitement which had thrilled
Me so completely when, while growing up,

I went on Saturdays to match or fight.
Not only me; for thousands of us there
Strode forward eagerly, each man aware
Of tingling memory, anticipating delight.

We all marched forward, all, except one man.
I saw him because he was paradoxically still,
A stone against the flood, face upright against us all,
Head bare, hoarse voice aloft, blind as a stone.

I knew him at once, despite his pathetic clothes;
Something in his stance, or his sturdy frame
Perhaps. I could even remember his name
Before I saw it on his blind-man's tray. Billy Rose.

And twenty forgetful years fell away at the sight.
Bare-kneed, dismayed, memory fled to the hub
Of Saturday violence, with friends to the Labour Club,
Watching the boxing on a sawdust summer night.

The boys' enclosure close to the shabby ring
Was where we stood, clenched in a resin world,
Spoke in cool voices, lounged, were artificially bored
During minor bouts. We paid threepence to go in.

Billy Rose fought there. He was top of the bill.
So brisk a fighter, so gallant, so precise!
Trim as a tree he stood for the ceremonies,
Then turned to meet George Morgan of Tirphil.

He had no chance. Courage was not enough,
Nor tight defence. Donald Davies was sick
And we threatened his cowardice with an embarrassed kick.
Ripped across both his eyes was Rose, but we were tough

And clapped him as they wrapped his blindness up
In busy towels, applauded the wave
He gave his executioners, cheered the brave
Blind man as he cleared with a jaunty hop

The top rope. I had forgotten that day
As if it were dead for ever, yet now I saw
The flowers of punched blood on the ring floor,
As bright as his name. I do not know

How long I stood with ghosts of the wild fists
And the cries of shaken boys long dead around me,
For struck to act at last, in terror and pity
I threw some frantic money, three treacherous pence –

And I cry at the memory – into his tray, and ran,
Entering the waves of the stadium like a drowning man.
Poor Billy Rose. God, he could fight
Before my three sharp coins knocked out his sight.

Early frost

We were warned about frost, yet all day the summer
Has wavered its heat above the empty stubble. Late
Bees hung their blunt weight,
Plump drops between those simplest wings, their leisure
An ignorance of frost.
My mind is full of the images of summer
And a liquid curlew calls from alps of air;

But the frost has come. Already under trees
Pockets of summer are dying, wide paths
Of the cold glow clean through the stricken thickets
And again I feel on my cheek the cut of winters
Dead. Once I awoke in a dark beyond moths
To a world still with freezing,
Hearing my father go to the yard for his ponies,

His hands full of frostnails to point their sliding
To a safe haul. I went to school,
Socks pulled over shoes for the streets' clear glass,
The early shops cautious, the tall
Classroom windows engraved by winter's chisel,
Fern, feather and flower that would not let the pale
Day through. We wrote in a cold fever for the morning

Play. Then boys in the exulting yard, ringing
Boots hard on winter, slapped with their polishing
Caps the arrows of their gliding, in steaming lines
Ran till they launched one by one
On the skills of ice their frail balance,
Sliding through time with not a fall in mind,
Their voices crying freely through such shouting

As the cold divided. I slid in the depth
Of the season till the swung bell sang us in.
Now insidious frost, its parched grains rubbing
At crannies, moved on our skin.
Our fingers died. Not the warmth
Of all my eight wide summers could keep me smiling.
The circle of the popping stove fell still
And we were early sped through the hurrying dark.

I ran through the bitterness on legs
That might have been brittle, my breath
Solid, grasping at stabs of bleak
Pain to gasp on. Winter branched in me, ice cracked
In my bleeding. When I fell through the teeth
Of the cold at my haven door I could not see

For locked tears, I could not feel the spent
Plenty of flames banked at the range,
Nor my father's hands as they roughed the blue
Of my knees. But I knew what he meant
With the love of his rueful laugh, and my true
World unfroze in a flood of happy crying,
As hot on my cheek as the sting of this present

Frost. I have stood too long in the orderly
Cold of the garden, I would not have again the death
Of that day come unasked as the comfortless dusk
Past the stakes of my fences. Yet these are my
Ghosts, they do not need to ask
For housing when the early frost comes down.
I take them in, all, to the settled warmth.

Siencyn ap Nicolas upon his death bed

Well, we all come to it. Siencyn, listen
to their cringing philosophies as the tears glisten
in the eyes of your punctual mourners.
I wish a plague would fasten

their plump hides to my stale bed!
But anger will never lift my head
again from this foul pillow.
I have learned tolerance, that soft word,

however unwillingly. It is one of my late.
one of my few, virtues. I hate
the hypocrite who takes a pleasure
in his honesty. Many a desolate

truth I've undone with a kind
lie. And hope to be forgiven. We can't stand
all kinds of truth. If God calls for my
account I must ask Him to turn a blind

eye to truth's ledgers, for there
I have no credit. When I spare
time for plain speaking I make sure
I'm not believed. There is a wild humour

in the accidental, savage truth I use
that makes it fictional. Old men can choose
a kind of general truth that turns to wisdom,
being void of malice. Not my way. But I'd not lose

a chance nobility I might, like a burr,
have picked on any casual road or moor
I've walked in my time. I'll not claim
merit for it. God's will. Found, not worked for.

Straight paths were never mine. When I was young
I let the hot blood take me where it stung.
God's doing, surely? He must know
His beautiful youths. I felt the sun

rise in my flushed veins, for the hot south
of life was in me and the songs my mouth
made then were many and easy. All roads
were mine for the laughing, and taking a breath

was like drinking wine. Yes, I remember
days when my five electric senses burned so clear
that I saw pale rainbows circumscribe the moon,
heard audible butterflies beat upon the air.

And the people I knew! A bright harmless
young man has friends everywhere. I witness
now that there was warmth on all the roads
for fifty miles and laughter in the villages

when I entered. And gave no thought to.
What's thought when the eager young are at their play?
Twin-faced I followed every tempting bend
alone on the ecstatic hills, or roaring in company.

I eased my ways through the lanes, and the taverns
knew me well. Slept nights in the tall ferns
and laughed in the dark. Groped awake
in the smart mornings and ran to the barns.

Then, one evening, I felt myself taken,
my legs not my own, afraid and shaken
by an apprehension of power beyond
all I could guess, to a path on the mountain

where climbing through rowan and bracken –
I see it all still – I came to a broken
and absolute crest. In the world beneath
the bright farms went to sleep, and the moon

began in splendour her processional ceremony.
This was how I was called to my craft. I knew
from that moment that all must be seen and said,
that words not mine would seem to be

mine. I climbed the hill alone and left alone,
yet all around me tree and beast and stone
moved as I moved. The wary twigs stared.
Feathers of birds rooted at my shoulder-bone.

So I have walked the hills for what might have been lost.
I have seen the sun walk drenched out of the mist
of early morning, and dance on the hill-top. I have
been old as a stone the lichen has soundlessly kissed

and known all enduring life in inanimate things.
I have left my body and grasped the soft rungs
of the air. Trees and grasses live in me,
through me the long-dead sing again their songs.

Is this not Heaven? Yes, it is mine.
And therefore true. I was always one of Aristotle's men
for whom the ideal good is never pure
abstraction. We make our images warm, human,

looking on our own distortions kindly.
But I'll not reject any sly hope of a friendly
Heaven to come. Not that I've earned it.
No, I must enter by invitation only.

Now it is autumn and pigeons flock to the fields,
bald listless blackbirds lurk in the muddy laurels
and the heavy geese drive their high, frail wedges
into an iron sky. The birds are restless,

as I am restless, held in a filthy
cage of flesh, an old, sick, man in a healthy
place, living his last on a rich son's
ready charity. Now in this wealthy

home I lie on a generous bed and feel
my life slide. I have sent away the girl
who came to read to me. To the young
nothing is simple. Why should my carrion smell

infect her innocence? Or my withered arm
misuse her compassion? Outside my room
the black weepers await my last
action. The ominous birds fly home.

And I must make my one way from
this shrivelled house of bones. I'll not welcome
Death, except in the way of courtesy.
I've loved in the world too long. But let him come.

Henry Treece   1921-66

The crimson cherry tree

There is no sweeter sight, I swear, in Heaven
Than blossom on the cherry trees by Clee.
Ah dainty brides, you dance on through my dreams
And in the town bring memory of a breeze
That blew from Corvedale, across the valley that
Must have run red with agony when Owen spoke,
Torturing the air about his council-chair
With shapes of fiery dragons flaming, wolves
That ran through city gates to bring despair
Upon the tow-haired marchers, tearing sheep
And leaving foul the water-holes. I feel
The failure of a people when that wind
Howls through my heart and shows me Caradoc
Heaped high with lads who should have brought their songs
Right to the walls of Ludlow, over Severn,
Regaining the green pastures with a word.

Ah, cherry-tree, so lissom in the wind,
Matter for poets and the love-sick mad,
I see your virgin blossom splashed with blood,
Bright red against the white, and at your feet
The gentle lord who walked without a sword,
Believing tales of peace among the hills,
Trusting the word, the signatory name,
Forgetting the black seasons of a race.

Second coming 1942

Under the hill the old horse stands
Away from the wind,
Waiting a second coming.
The timid flock together by the wall
Cough and slip back into their dream
Of meadow-lands where knife was never known.

The old man clasps his tired hands
And seems to find
No labour worth the doing.
The rusty bucket jangles at the well,
And memories rush into the room
Of the lost son who is to be reborn.

Y Ddraig Goch

The dragon of our dreams roared in the hills
That ring the sunlit land of children's songs.
Red with the lacquer of a fairy-tale,
His fiery breath fried all besieging knights.
Whole seasons could he lay the land in waste
By puffing once upon the standing corn!

He was our dragon dressed in red, who kept
Sly ghosts from lurking underneath the thatch,
And made the hen lay dark-brown eggs for tea.
One word to him, just as you went to bed,
Made Twm, the postman, call next afternoon;
'Ho, bachgen', That is what he'd say, 'Just look,
A fine blue postal-order from your Mam!
Twm gets a pint for bring that, I bet!'

The dragon cured us when the measles came,
And let the mare drop me a coal-black foal.
He taught us where nests lay, and found us fish,
Then thawed the snow to save the winter lamb.

Ho, Ddraig Goch, my pretty, pretty friend!
We were his children, knowing all his ways;
We laid out nightly gifts beneath the hedge,
Five linnet's eggs, a cup, a broken whip,
And heard his gracious sighs sweep through the trees.
But tears for all the fools who called him false!
One lad who sniggered fell down Parry's well;
The English Parson had a plague of warts;
Old Mrs Hughes was bitten by a cat;
The school roof fell in when the teacher smiled!

Ho, Ddraig Goch, they tell me you are dead;
They say they heard you weeping in the hills
For all your children gone to London Town.
They say your tears set Tawe in a flood.
I'm older now, but still I like to think
Of your great glass-green eyes fixed on the Fferm,
Guarding the children, keeping them from harm.

Don't die, old dragon, wait a few years more,
I shall come back and bring you boys to love.

Robert Morgan   b. 1921

The carpenter

One

I survey my garden neglected
For the labour of words. The daffodils
Are shrunken, bowing with the weight
Of faded spring and reminding me of time.
A sparrow pecks at a compost
Heap, a thrush, stone still,
Longs for turned earth,
Sycamore trees clap their leaves
And tremble with a dialogue of air.
Above my fence a blind window
Shades a quiet room where
A carpenter lies dying.
Yesterday I sat in his Victorian room
And we worked our gardens with words
And brought back the summer gone.
We pretended time was unrationed
While time's shadow inched
Away from his oak face.

Two

He is not aware of my soliloquy
Under his window, only the weight
Of his bones and a slow drip
Of memory down the aisle of his mind.
I see his flowers are brighter than mine,
His hedges straighter and his lawns
Smooth evidence of skillripe hands.
The sun feeds his flock of flowers,
May beans are climbing,
But a green tide of weed
Has begun to move in.

Three

Tomorrow I will mow my lawns
And weed and cut the dead daffodils
And report my progress to the man
On his bed of broken dreams.
He will talk like dry, rustling leaves
And I will pretend and he will pretend
And we will act it out together
To a background of birds, children,
Dogs and motor cars; but when
Will it end, all this walking about
Quietly, remembering how I used to borrow
His tools, his skills, the cups of tea
On his homemade garden oak seat
And his snowy wife, busy, proud
And Christian, all this waiting
And watching on the shore of his window.

Four

The irises are out, reminding me
Of Van Gogh, his bandaged head,
His red beard and the Arles sun.
And this sky, a child's symbol
Of Heaven and eternal blue,
Drenches with light and warmth
As the carpenter slips away, among
The flowers of his last season.

Peter Hellings   b. 1922

Academic festival

1 Congregation of the Waters

The crowds flow in, dull floods along dry channels
In midsummer.
          Splashes of recognition
Flatter, and humour and chatter without intermission
Raise a heard rumour under symbolic panels
Pinker than life, an empire scoured of fleas,
Indecently riotous for daylight.
              Still they stream
Dazing the ushers to a fish-dark dream
With furious little rivers and big tributaries
Assembling into a lake of ruffled conjecture:
When are the prizes, when will we see our son
Rewarded, slaving and labour done, and the lecture
Be read, and the praises,
              when will we see our daughter
Ascend the dais,
          not as of old for the slaughter,
But flowerless, and clad in black, and with all her clothes on . . .

2 Entry of the Pedagogues

This is a silent splendour. The crowd stands.
Here are no drums and trumpets, paraphernalia
Of power, attendant sandwich-men and bands,
Strumpets and bums – that would indeed be a failure
Of tact, to those whom we owe respect.

They come
Heralded by the thunder of their feet
On carpet, twisted heads and curious hum
Of those standing and waiting in awe to greet
The black gowns bellowing silently, the blare
Of scarlet hoods, green facings trimmed with fur
Mounting the stage as furtively as they dare
Wearing disguise:
                    for well they know the stir
These soundless trumpetings arouse, and therefore
Uneasily wear them like the trumpery of a whore.

3 Honoured in Welsh

The court and senate seated, and each new graduate
Honoured in Welsh.
                    But here's no dragon fire
Of eloquence, though the Welsh tongue's a great
Conjuror, and can set a flag on fire
As at Llyn, Carmarthenshire, and still carries great weight
And is even lovelier sung.
                    But there's no choir,
The Chairs are harder and more forbidding of late
Lamented professors, and each new bard is a liar
Boasting two tongues which always can be blended
But never completely divided. There lies our weakness.
The young man lifts his head:
                    There is a sickness
Asleep in the soil, where tongues, like roots are tended.
Our birth with the world's blood was tainted,
                                                so
Pure Welsh is a dark flower we failed to grow.

4 Invocation to the Mastersinger

Polite applause flies up, a flight of pigeons
Scattered by handclaps' rapid rifle fire
That sends this tame praise sweeping round a spire
To settle again, like faiths and dead religions,
And sunlit dust.
     For whom is this applause
But that mediaeval image on the stage,
A burning, stooping, gaunt dark man, who draws
Over his sober coat the heritage
And air of timelessness,
       as if he walked
Clear out of context, and had at his bed's head
Twenty volumes of Aristotle bound in red
And handsome black,
       yet softly swore, and talked
Despite degree, to any man, and wore
The smiling irony of the learned poor.

5 Dance of the Apprentices

There is a sound of revelry, and bright
Eyes mirror lights, and at last trumpets sound:
Intelligent conversations, and the trite
War records worn with repetition, drowned
In clattering glasses, swiftly degenerate
To a ghost's memory shot with lust and beer
And lashed with laughter, in which we celebrate
Forgotten triumphs and unconquered fear,
A different fellowship.
      In the past we were
Apprentices to another war, yet here
With all illusions lost, we would prolong
Victories time has reversed:
       the old
Are scrupulously romantic, while the young
Though cynical, are tremulously bold.

Dannie Abse   b. 1923

The game

Follow the crowds to where the turnstiles click.
The terraces fill. *Hoompa*, blares the brassy band.
Saturday afternoon has come to Ninian Park
and, beyond the goalposts, in the Canton Stand
between black spaces, a hundred matches spark.

Waiting, we recall records, legendary scores:
Fred Keenor, Hardy, in a royal blue shirt.
The very names, sad as the old songs, open doors
before our time where someone else was hurt.
Now, like an injured beast, the great crowd roars.

The coin is spun. Here all is simplified
and we are partisan who cheer the Good,
hiss at passing Evil. Was Lucifer offside?
A wing falls down when cherubs howl for blood.
Demons have agents: the Referee is bribed.

The white ball smacked the crossbar. Satan rose
higher than the others in the smoked brown gloom
to sink on grass in a ballet dancer's pose.
Again, it seems, we hear a familiar tune
not quite identifiable. A distant whistle blows.

Memory of faded games, the discarded years;
talk of Aston Villa, Orient, and the Swans.
Half-time, the band played the same military airs
as when The Bluebirds once were champions.
Round touchlines, the same cripples in their chairs.

Mephistopheles had his joke. The honest team
dribbles ineffectually, no one can be blamed.
Infernal backs tackle, inside forwards scheme,
and if they foul us need we be ashamed?
Heads up! Oh for a Ted Drake, a Dixie Dean.

'Saved' or else, discontents, we are transferred
long decades back, like Faust must pay that fee.
The Night is early. Great phantoms in us stir
as coloured jerseys hover, move diagonally
on the damp turf, and our eidetic visions blur.

God sign our souls! Because the obscure Staff
of Hell rule this world, jugular fans guessed
the result halfway through the second half,
and those who know the score just seem depressed.
Small boys swarm the field for an autograph.

Silent the Stadium. The crowds have all filed out.
Only the pigeons beneath the roofs remain.
The clean programmes are trampled underfoot,
and natural the dark, appropriate the rain,
whilst, under lamp-posts, threatening newsboys shout.

Odd

In front of our house in Golders Green
the lawn, like a cliché, mutters 'Rose bushes'.
The whole suburb is very respectable.
Ugly men drive past in funeral suits,
from their necks you can tell they're overweight.

Sodium lamp-posts, at night, hose empty roads
with gold which treacles over pavement trees,
polishes brittle hedges, clings on closed, parked cars.
If a light should fly on in an upstairs room
odds on two someones are going to sleep.

It's unusual to meet a beggar,
you hardly ever see a someone drunk.
It's a nice, clean, quiet, religious place.
For my part, now and then, I want to scream;
thus, by the neighbours, am considered odd.

From the sensible wastes of Golders Green
I journey to Soho where a job owns me.
Soho is not a respectable place.
Underweight women in the gamiest of skirts
bleed a smile of false teeth at ugly men.

Later, the dark is shabby with paste electric
of peeporamas, brothels, clubs and pubs,
restaurants that sport sallow waiters who cough.
If a light should fly on in an upstairs room
odds on two someones are going to bed.

It's customary to see many beggars,
common to meet people roaring and drunk.
It's a nice, loud, dirty, irreligious place.
For my part, now and then, I want to scream;
thus, by Soho friends, am considered odd.

The French master

Everyone in Class II at the Grammar School
had heard of Walter Bird, known as Wazo.
They said he'd behead each dullard and fool
or, instead, carve off a tail for the fun.

Wazo's cane buzzed like a bee in the air.
Quietly, quietly, in the desks of Form III
sneaky Wazo tweaked our ears and our hair.
Walter Wazo, public enemy No. 1.

Five feet tall, he married sweet Doreen Wall
and combmarks furrowed his vaselined hair;
his hands still fluttered ridiculously small,
his eyes the colour of a poison bottle.

Who'd think he'd falter, poor love-sick Walter
as bored he read out *Lettres de mon Moulin*;
his mouth had begun to soften and alter,
and Class IV ribbed him as only boys can.

Perhaps through kissing his wife to a moan
had alone changed the shape of his lips,
till the habit of her mouth became his own:
no more Walter Wazo, enemy No. 1.

'Boy' he'd whine, 'yes, please decline the verb to have,'
in tones dulcet and mild as a girl.
'Sorry sir, can't sir, must go to the lav,'
whilst Wazo stared out of this world.

Till one day in May Wazo buzzed like a bee
and stung, twice, many a warm, inky hand;
he stormed through the form, a catastrophe,
returned to this world, No. 1.

Alas, alas, to the Vth Form's disgrace
nobody could quote Villon to that villain.
Again the nasty old mouth zipped on his face,
and not a weak-bladdered boy in the class.

Was Doreen being kissed by a Mr Anon?
Years later, I purred, 'Your dear wife, Mr Bird?'
teeth bared, how he *glared* before stamping on;
and suddenly I felt sorry for the bastard.

Return to Cardiff

'Hometown'; well, most admit an affection for a city:
grey, tangled streets I cycled on to school, my first cigarette
in the back lane, and, fool, my first botched love affair.
First everything. Faded torments; self-indulgent pity.

The journey to Cardiff seemed less a return than a raid
on mislaid identities. Of course the whole locus smaller:
the mile-wide Taff now a stream, the castle not as in some black,
gothic dream, but a decent sprawl, a joker's toy façade.

Unfocused voices in the wind, associations, clues,
odds and ends, fringes caught, as when, after the doctor quit,
a door opened and I glimpsed the white, enormous face
of my grandfather, suddenly aghast with certain news.

Unable to define anything I can hardly speak,
and still I love the place for what I wanted it to be
as much as for what it unashamedly is
now for me, a city of strangers, alien and bleak.

Unable to communicate I'm easily betrayed,
uneasily diverted by mere sense reflections
like those anchored waterscapes that wander, alter, in the Taff,
hour by hour, as light slants down a different shade.

Illusory, too, that lost dark playground after rain,
the noise of trams, gunshots in what they once called Tiger Bay.
Only real this smell of ripe, damp earth when the sun comes out,
a mixture of pungencies, half exquisite and half plain.

No sooner than I'd arrived the other Cardiff had gone,
smoke in the memory, these but tinned resemblances,
where the boy I was not and the man I am not
met, hesitated, left double footsteps, then walked on.

Epithalamion

Singing, today I married my white girl
beautiful in a barley field.
Green on thy finger a grass blade curled,
so with this ring I thee wed, I thee wed,
and send our love to the loveless world
of all the living and all the dead.

Now, no more than vulnerable human,
we, more than one, less than two,
are nearly ourselves in a barley field –
and only love is the rent that's due
though the bailiffs of time return anew
to all the living but not the dead.

Shipwrecked, the sun sinks down harbours
of a sky, unloads its liquid cargoes
of marigolds, and I and my white girl
lie still in the barley – who else wishes
to speak, what more can be said
by all the living against all the dead?

Come then all you wedding guests:
green ghost of trees, gold of barley,
you blackbird priests in the field,
you wind that shakes the pansy head
fluttering on a stalk like a butterfly;
come the living and come the dead.

Listen flowers, birds, winds, worlds,
tell all today that I married
more than a white girl in the barley –
for today I took to my human bed
flower and bird and wind and world,
and all the living and all the dead.

Letter to Alex Comfort

Alex, perhaps a colour of which neither of us had dreamt
may appear in the test-tube with God knows what admonition.
Ehrlich certainly was one who broke down the mental doors,
yet only after his six hundred and sixth attempt.

Koch also, painfully, and with true German thoroughness,
eliminated the impossible to prove that too many of us
are dying from the same disease. Visible, on the slide
at last – Death – and the thin bacilli of an ancient distress.

Still I, myself, don't like Germans, but prefer the unkempt
voyagers, who, like butterflies drunk with suns,
can only totter crookedly in the dazed air
to reach charmingly their destination, as if by accident.

That Greek one, then, is my hero, who watched the bath water
rise above his navel and rushed out naked, 'I found it,
I found it' into the street in all his shining, and forgot
that others would only stare at his genitals. What laughter!

Or Newton, leaning in Woolsthorpe against the garden wall,
forgot his indigestion and all such trivialities,
but gaped up at heaven in just surprise, and with
true gravity, witnessed the vertical apple fall.

O what a marvellous observation! Who would have reckoned
that such a pedestrian miracle could alter history,
that, henceforward, everyone must fall, whatever
their rank, at thirty-two feet per second, per second?

You too, I know, have waited for doors to fly open, played
with your cold chemicals and written long letters
to the Press; listened to the truth afraid and dug deep
into the wriggling earth for a rainbow, with an honest spade.

But nothing rises. Neither spectres, nor oil, nor love.
And the old professor must think you mad, Alex, as you rehearse
poems in the laboratory like vows, and curse those clever scientists
who dissect away the wings and haggard heart from the dove.

John Ormond   b. 1923

Design for a tomb

Dwell in this stone who once was tenant of flesh.
Alas, lady, the phantasmagoria is over,
Your smile must come to terms with dark for ever.

Carved emblems, puff-cheeked cherubs and full vines
Buoy up your white memorial in the chapel,
Weightlessly over you who welcomed a little weight.

Lie unprotesting who often lay in the dark,
Once trembling switchback lady keep your stillness
Lest marble crack, ornate devices tumble.

Old melodies were loth to leave your limbs.
Love's deft reluctances where many murmured delight
Lost all their gay glissandi, grew thin and spare

Between a few faint notes. Your bright fever
Turned towards cold, echoed remembered sweets.
Those who for years easily climbed to your casement

Left by the tall front hall. Lust grown respectable
Waltzed slow knight's moves under the portico,
Crabbed in a black gown. You were carried out

Feet first, on your back, still, over the broad chequers.
So set up slender piers, maidenhair stone
Like green fern springing again between ivory oaks,

The four main pillars to your canopy;
And underneath it, up near the cornices
Set in small fenestrations to catch the light

152

That still chinks, spy-holing the bent laurel
With worn footholds outside your bedroom window
Through which you'd hear an early gardener's hoe

Chivvy the weeds edging the gravel path
Then turn dazedly into your lover's arms
Fumbling to doze back, calling the morning false.

Lady-lust, so arranged in ornamental bed,
Baring your teeth for the first apple of heaven,
Juices and sap still run. Sleep well-remembered.

Cathedral builders

They climbed on sketchy ladders towards God,
With winch and pulley hoisted hewn rock into heaven,
Inhabited sky with hammers, defied gravity,
Deified stone, took up God's house to meet Him,

And came down to their suppers and small beer;
Every night slept, lay with their smelly wives,
Quarrelled and cuffed the children, lied,
Spat, sang, were happy or unhappy

And every day took to the ladders again;
Impeded the rights of way of another summer's
Swallows; grew greyer, shakier, became less inclined
To fix a neighbour's roof of a fine evening;

Saw naves sprout arches, clerestories soar,
Cursed the loud fancy glaziers for their luck,
Somehow escaped the plague, got rheumatism,
Decided it was time to give it up,

To leave the spire to others; stood in the crowd
Well back from the vestments at the consecration,
Envied the fat bishop his warm boots,
Cocked up a squint eye and said, 'I bloody did that.'

Instructions to settlers

who arrived in Patagonia from Wales 1865

On these lean shelves of land
Nothing but thorn thrives.
At noon cross-winds foregather
To suck and subdivide
The dust and the white sand
Between one shelf and another.
With thornstumps then mark out
The plots for your bent lives.
This place is home. Possess
The wilderness with yourselves,
Dig deep. Cut down to zero,
Cut through land's wasted face
To where springs bitter with brine
Pulse side-long and in vain
Under the restless dust,
Under the wind-worn plain;
And through the coarsest thorn
Strike with sharp dream, sharp bone
To reach brief union
With this mistaken Canaan.
Search here where seed was lost,
Work stone and white to green
And ease your tormented ghost.

Alison J. Bielski   b. 1925

The Thigh Stone

One

How could this stone, thigh smooth,
return to its niche in crumbling walls
of its own accord, when stolen away?

Yesterday, in the ruined church
of Llaniden on windy Menai shores,

we saw the place where it lay
cemented. Your yellow hair blazed

out of darkness, raindrops linked
long strands over your upturned

collar. We thought of iron chains
binding the Thigh Stone to another,

when both were hurled into green
waves, to see if it would return
again. But we did not envy its

ancient fame. Standing hands
clasped, we pitied its immobility.

Two

Today we plunge into rough sea,
chained together by links of light.

You turn, tossing salt spray,
suddenly leap out of waves,
trample rough shingle, disappear.

You have climbed back into your
niche in the wall, embryo curled,

irremovable as the Thigh Stone,
carved eyelids closed, sleeping
cemented into your hiding-place.

Three

I swim alone. What fierce power
snatched your sea-cold hands from mine?

We are separated. Broken chains
cannot fathom your mystery, you
are invisible, merged in rock.

I cannot exist without you.
Sinking slowly,
                    I drown in a ruined sea.

Raymond Garlick   b. 1926

Vowels

A
is life,
a sharp grass ray
green as the apple that Adam's wife
plucked from the spray
that leaf-rife
day.

E
is you,
the golden key
turning the verbs forever through
a praxis with to be:
who construe
me.

I
is man,
erect in the sky,
a charcoal hieroglyph sketched to span
thesis and thigh,
to plant, plan,
die.

O
is God,
the calm rondeau
round which the constellations plod,
an ivory glow
of untrod
snow.

U
is space,
Picasso blue,
through which, like great birds in their grace
sweeping the world's fresh dew,
words chase
you.

Note on the Iliad

Why are epics
always about
the anti-life
of a noble lout?

I sing Lely
who burnt no tower
but brought the sea-floor
into flower.

Imagine it –
the moment when
out of the
architectured fen

the polder surfaced
sleek as a whale
and still awash.
Then the last veil

of standing water
slides away.
Glistening land
like a wet tray

serves up its past,
wreck upon wreck
glazed in the sand
of this smooth deck:

like Ararat,
the antique shores
ride up again
ready for Noahs.

Now wheat ripples
where schooner and barque
thrashed down the waters
to ultimate dark –

avenued Holland
waves over plains
which twenty years back
rocked fishing-seines.

Hard to imagine
the North Sea floor
was where we picnic –
and even more

to imagine this:
a people at grips
with genesis
not apocalypse.

Capitals

Moscow,
like a Christmas-tree,
glisters on the linen snow.
Fabergé red stars filigree
the mast-high spires, glitter and flow
over the square's starched sea
below.

Madrid,
a fortress on a height,
chessboard of stone, a granite grid
lifted and spread to the lancing light
staring down from the sun's arched lid:
of Europe's cities knight
and Cid.

Dublin
in a Yeatsian haze,
Liffey waters strong as gin,
back-streets like a Chinese maze,
and Trinity, a palanquin –
the Book of Kells ablaze
within.

And Rome,
the white and marble rose
of Europe, rising from the foam
of all the fountains art unfroze
from conduits in time's catacomb:
which in their spray disclose
the dome.

Paris,
and the Seine's long psalm
holding in parenthesis
hundred-tapered Notre Dame –
pavilion of the genesis
of joy, and heaven's calm
chrysalis.

And Bonn,
empalaced on the Rhine,
where Beethoven looked out upon
symphonic counties-palatine.
Over river, bridge and swan
that fierce gaze, leonine,
once shone.

Cardiff
swirls about the numb
and calm cube of its castle cliff:
rune of departed power for some
to others towers a hieroglyph
of sovereign power to come
if if.

And last,
sun-ambered Amsterdam –
the churning hurdy-gurdy's blast
chiming with carillon and tram:
canal and concrete here contrast
their tenses, and enjamb
the past.

Europe:
young Ap Iwan's yard,
Gruffydd Robert's vision's scope,
Morgan Llwyd's hoist petard:
source to which our ballads grope –
context, compass-card
and hope.

Blaenau observed (extract)

Scene two. Interior of the town's main school.
The stage is furnished with twelve boys in desks;
one master, gowned; one master's dais and stool.

High in my classroom here, upon the edge
of school and town and precipice, I look
down through my windows, past the low-walled ledge

of school yard, past the palisade of pines,
down to the canyon of Cwm Bowydd deep
below – a trough of mist fluffing the lines

of river and wood. Up here all is fair
in the apricot, nine o'clock sunlight
and the waking morning and the washed air.

To the left, the valley: to the right, the town:
and between them five moments, white and still,
before bells jangle the silence down

and desks jerk open and the day begins.
But for five calm minutes the world sits still
while the wheel of imagination spins.

And sometimes in its turning I can hear
the ring of feet upon a street in Troy
and Helen singing as she braids her hair,

or Socrates in some suburban shop
unlock the logos to Athenian ears;
– hear Hywel of Deheubarth leave his ship

and ride with harpists into holy Rome.
Soon, far from home in some brash Oxford tower,
Ieuan ap Hywel Swrdwal maps a rhyme

and flaps swan wings and sings in English verse.
In the city of Deiniol Shakespeare invests
the Archdeacon's House with Glendower's voice.

Now Gruffydd Robert, canon of Milan,
sets down his Grammar on the window seat
and seems to hear Welsh voices in the lane.

Now Owain Myfyr stitches at a ream
of yellow furs and Iolo manuscripts
– his four-walled Wales a London sewing-room,

Civitas, civitatis – a large town,
a city, *dinas*: this great symphony
of tones and tongues used not to be our tune.

There we were always exiles—quick to seize
(or sell) our bread amid the alien corn;
and yet Saint David's city was our size:

cathedral, village inn, a house or two,
a crumbling palace and a claim to fame
– the church for emptiness, the inn for tea.

Our life was mountain-boned and fleshed with fields.
We were at home upon the lonely hills
– with flocks of sheep, not men, crowding the folds.

We were not city folk. Within our walls,
fronting the piazza or boulevard,
the kettled firelight lit a little Wales:

knocker and door-knob kneaded, steps blenched clean,
new polished parlour, candlesticks aglint,
and 'Salem' on the wall – all as in Llan.

Time turns; the centuries sift and die.
Soft as snow petals on the valley floor
drift up the sounds of cities of today:

cities of Wales, planted in parks and plans
that rationalize the black and twisted towns
called down by coal upon the wheat-green plains.

I hear the patter of Saturday sounds
in Swansea market – cockle women's cries
and laver sellers', salty as the sands,

and sharp as winds that bite Carmarthen bays;
the angelus at noon; Salvation bands
and football armies; shouts of corner-boys.

The canticle of Cardiff – from the roar
of Tigers in the Bay to crack of ball
on bat; and that most gracious sound (most rare) –

the gasp of children at new rooms of life
thrown open – art, antiquity: the heart
laid bare upon the fragile, living leaf.

John Tripp   b. 1927

Lincoln, 1301

A divine slaps a small tin thing
on young Edward's skull, and so begins
the damp farce of royal yoke.
Now through thirty peculiar reigns,
chipped sculpted heads of monarchs
will fringe the roof of Llandaff;
chill charity of corpulent satraps,
wedged fat on their mouldy thrones,
will shut off tomorrow in this province
disputed since Caradoc's time.

The crown's lop-sided on the baffled lad
who will squat for twenty years
                          as king of nothing.
Think of the yards of parchment,
the drip of the red wax seals
to stream the keen expeditions out
                          to collapse the Welsh!

But one generation dilutes its valour
into the next: soon the Fluellens flock
to Monmouth's banner, for a coin a day they are fodder
for a noble speech.

As a nation sinks into torpor,
one heir is topped with the tin at Caernarfon
and motors to see dead Dowlais,
                    with his lady back at the fort.
(His princely apparel crusts with dust
                    in our bleak museum.)
Seven centuries distant from Lincoln,
in the swarming capital of the Welsh,
the latest incumbent is cheered
                    on a rugby field!

The diesel to yesterday

There is downpour, always,
    as the carriages inch into Newport:
perhaps six times in ten years
    of a hundred visits to custom,
the entry to my country is uncurtained
    by rain or mist. I look
at the shambles of sidings and streets,
    the rust of progress and freight wagons,
the cracked façades of bingo cinemas.
    Sometimes I expect to see
the callous peaked caps and buttons
    of visa-checkers, cold sentries
on a foreign border, keeping out the bacillus
    in hammering rain and swirling fog.
Often I wish it were so, this frontier sealed
    at Chepstow, against frivolous incursion
from the tainting eastern zones.

Patience vanishes with frayed goodwill
   at the sight of the plump bundles
tumbling into Wales.
   They bring only their banknotes
and a petrol-stenched lust for scenery
   to shut in their kodaks,
packing out the albums of Jersey
   and the anthill beaches of the south.
They stand in line for pre-heated grease
   in the slums of crumbled resorts,
nose their long cars into pastureland
   and the hearts of ancient townships
that now are buried under chromium plate.

I catch myself out in error, feel
   ignoble in disdain.
The bad smell at my nostril
   is some odour from myself –
a modern who reeks of the museum,
   not wanting his own closed yesterday
but the day before that,
   the lost day before dignity went,
when all our borders were sealed.

Welcome to Wales

You drive in across this bridge they've built
or sleep through the railway tunnel
or step from a shaky plane on the coast.
The roads are quite modern, and the beer
is warm and generally flat.
The clocks keep the same time as Surbiton.

Our places of worship are more numerous
than the crumbling pubs, but their thin congregations
stay in bed. We have no
monopoly of compassion, but believe
no distance is too excessive
from a cold heart. Our schools
are full of children, and our seats of learning
turn out the usual quota of misfits.

Among the ancient customs, buttering-up tourists
is not one, so beware of the remnant of pride
hanging in corners. If you prick us,
we shall surely bleed. Here you can buy
what you purchase in Selfridges
and cut a small notch in your wallet for every snip.
There are plenty of bogus Tudor
expense-account restaurants; the hotels bulge
with rugby players, their supporters still happily dissecting
a try scored in 1912.
You will feel at home in the petrol fumes.

Our women are full and bloomy,
real women. Our girls
shuttle nicely in micro skirts.
(They are always a shock to the stranger.)

Our complaint is apathy, which would not
interest the visitor hungry for landscape.
We are not sure who we are, but the search
goes on. Experts fly in from abroad
to write big books about us,
to tell us who we are.

There's a splendid ritual in August
(swot up on the language first)
and singing high in the north
(book well in advance for your beds)
when the world comes rattling in motor cars
to our separate doorstep. You can eat
delicious flat cakes that are griddle-baked
and copy some recipes discovered in Caesar's time.
But our special flair is confusion: we have trouble
with our souls, and this could be tedious
if you bog yourself down in discourse
with local philosophers. On benches
in village squares, the very old keep chiselling memories.

But make no mistake, and mark this well:
we do not sell ourselves cheap,
or short, despite what the experts say.

Soliloquy for compatriots

We even have our own word for God
in a language nourished on hymn and psalm
as we clinched to our customs and habitats.
All those decades ago
in the chapels of the scarred zones,
lean clergymen made it quite clear
He had singled us out as his chosen.
He would care for the beaten Welsh people.
But now the strangers come to bang more nails
in the battered coffin of Wales.
                              Their sleek cars
slam up the passes and through the green vales,
the bramble shudders from the screaming exhausts.

A tangled image of pits and poverty,
Eisteddfodau and love on slag-heaps,
invades their haphazard minds.
Four hundred years of the king's writ
have not shaken their concept of our role:

                       foxy, feckless,
articulate, mercurial, lyrical and wild,
we are clogged with feeling,
ranting preachers on the rebellious fronde.

All our princes gone, betrayal and sack
ended in a seal on parchment.
Our follies have all been almanacked, and our bards
are piping on reeds where once the trumpets sounded.
Death is the ancient popular topic we nibble.

Inept, they say, like the Irish
we have fought too long for the crumbs
from rich men's tables.
               How could they know
for one moment of the steely wonder
of pride in legend in a sunken past,
the stiff stubborn strap to our backbone
that makes others still seek us out?

Douglas Phillips b. 1929

To Sir Lewis Morris

Excuse me, Sir Lewis, I hope you don't mind my addressing you
Directly, even though you almost became Poet Laureate, for I
Was born in the same town, looked at the same view
Over the Towy, but of course, unlike you, have yet to die.

Yes, we even went to the same school, though not on the same day;
Reading Tennyson's Idylls in a draughty classroom, how was I to guess
That he had many times walked with you along this way,
A guest, a fellow-poet, at your home address?

Unknowingly we rub shoulders with the great, their ghosts
Pass, invisible pedestrians on the pavement, we
Walk on, never realizing how close their muted behests.
We encounter our pasts daily; they nod unobtrusively.

Years later, reading a guide-book or local history, we awake
To the truth we denied when we slept. Too late to retrace
Our steps in those years when with dull opaque
Eyes all we saw was what the sense of sight showed to our face.

I must have passed you many times running down to the river,
A boy, to watch the dark coracles, or later arm-in-arm
With my first girl-friend. How could I ever
Have seen you, immune as I was to any imaginary muse's charm?

I apologize if I have invaded your privacy.
Impossible not to acknowledge you now I have grown
Up with some inexplicable interest in poetry, even though your residuary
Reputation is perhaps one you would not willingly own.

Even a Laureate is not necessarily a resident statue
In poetry's pantheon, so I should not grieve at being passed over.
You have your grave here on this hill. At least with a view
Like this beauty needs no shrine built by a purely verbal lover.

Even those umpteen editions of yours – twentieth or was it twenty-first?
Best-selling Epics of Hades, now consigned to second-hand shelves,
Gather dust as quietly as this evening veils with its mist
The bright sun setting of your unscanned second selves.

A knighthood, fame, an applauding audience, such were the fruits
Of the golden apples of your pre-Raphaelite Hesperides.
Accept my salutation, though scorn the implied roots
Of my pity. How could I condescend in face of such heydays as these?

Anthony Conran   b. 1931

Happiness

I did not find the plant, no, not for all my searching,
   Until a smile of yours led me to common ground
And in a copse of alders stooped, and by a stone
   Discovered to my wonder its blue of heart's content.

And now, wherever I look, so blind was I before,
   I see it common as bindweed, everywhere
A constant, lazy tune, like a brook or kettle
   As generally unnoticed as a piece of sky.

Perhaps, though, the flower grows best in the tough
   Peaty soil of a scarp or dell: you might find
A hare with its ears back, ready to run like wind,
   Or the peewits standing one-legged on its curling leaf.

Here, between noon and sunset, stray lovers may come
   And between them for a chain bruise filigree stalks
With each a chaste cluster of buds, one or two at a time
   Putting forth sudden blue for one livelong day.

And at dusk, shepherds whistle their dogs, pick the spray
   Idly, and their quiet wives find it in random nosegays
When the coat's off, and supper's away, and the fire
   Lullabies the gaunt man of the house to a dreamless sleep.

A crown for Anna Daniel

1 On the Road to Glasinfryn

We allowed the yellow-hammer's taunt
  And the blown rooks
To tempt us to trial
  Of Cloudcuckooland walks.

But came, every so often,
  To discover a well
Tucked with slate below wayside:
  The water was so still

That inch-cold centuries
  Halted our way
And we peered down in bewilderment
  Forgetting the bright day

In a trance of sudden calm
  Through which has moved
A bubble-hoarding beetle
  Since before Adam delved.

2 Swing-gate

Swing-gate, you called it; but to me
  The old name, kissing-gate
Stops an ironware gap in the hedge
With a more authentic smack
  Than any swing-gate.

A half-moon rail, almost a maze
  With its radial bar –
I suppose the kissing done
As the girl was caught
  Between arc and bar.

'Look there's the swing-gate!'
  'Kissing-gate', I said,
And watched you trust the name
As you pushed between arc and bar
  Quicken your free tread.

3 The Fledgling

Dark speckle, half with down, half feathered,
  A stump tail sprouted,
Wren fledgling sat in the road,
  Its flying just started.

Shut resolute eyes had achieved
  Two feet of flight;
It was too tired with that glory
  To feel any fright.

Blind tyre of a car might roll
  And rub out the fear
Of a world just glimpsed, just learnt,
  If we left it here.

I like the clumsiness of honest mercy
  With which you stoop
To free those incredibly long toes
  From the road's grip.

How another girl would dance
  In the picking it up –
Hold it to her like a babe,
  Ladybird, buttercup!

But I'm relieved you do not make it yours
  Like a casual thief:
Gravely you show it me, gravely lay it down
  Into private green leaf.

The fox

A furlong from the crest, when the bell's cry
Of hillbreast churches called us villageward,
And the sun, bright and unsetting in July,
Invited to the summits – suddenly stood
By step unwitting and delicate mute tread
A rare wonder before us, a red fox.
We did not move, even our breath stopped dead,
Paralysed utterly. Like three cold rocks

We stood. Then, at a careless crest of his stride,
He too froze dead, stunned for a moment there.
Above his poised foot, two flames, unflickering wide,
Gleamed of his eyes. Then, without haste or fear,
His dry red pelt slipped over the rock scar,
And was; and was not – like some shooting star.

Translated from the Welsh of R. Williams Parry   1884–1956

Rhydcymerau

Near Rhydcymerau,
On the land of Esgeir-ceir and the fields of Tir-bach,
They have planted the saplings
        to be trees for the third war.

I call to mind my grandmother at Esgeir-ceir
As she sat, pleating her apron, by the fireside,
The skin yellow and dry on her face
        like a manuscript of Peniarth,
And the Welsh on her old lips the Welsh of Pantycelyn.
A bit of the Puritan Wales she was of last century.
Although I never saw him, my grandfather
Was a 'character', a brisk and twinkling little creature,
Fond of his pint;
He'd just strayed in from the eighteenth century.
They reared nine children,
Poets, deacons, and Sunday School teachers,
And each, locally, a man of authority.

My Uncle Dafydd used to farm Tir-bach,
And was, besides, a poet, the countryside's rhymester;
His song to the little cockerel was famous in those parts:
        'The little cock goes scratching
         in the garden here and there.'
It was to him I went for the summer holidays
To watch the sheep and fashion lines of *cynghanedd*,
Englynion, and eight-line stanzas
        of eight-seven measure.
He brought up eight children,
The eldest son a minister with the Calvinistic Methodists,
And he too wrote verses.
In our family we'd a real nestful of poets.

And by this time there's nothing there but trees.
Impertinent roots suck dry the old soil:
Trees where neighbourhood was,
And a forest that once was farmland.
Where was verse-writing and scripture
                    is the South's bastardized English.
The fox barks where once cried lambs and children,
And there, in the dark midst,
Is the den of the English minotaur;
And on the trees, as if on crosses,
The bones of poets, deacons, ministers, and teachers of Sunday School
Bleach in the sun,
And the rain washes them, and the winds lick them dry.

Translated from the Welsh of D. Gwenallt Jones   1899–1968

In two fields

Weun Parc y Blawd and Parc y Blawd in Pembrokeshire.

Where did the sea of light roll from
Onto Flower Meadow Field and Flower Field?
After I'd searched for long in the dark land,
The one that was always, whence did he come?
Who, oh who was the marksman, the sudden enlightener?
The roller of the sea was the field's living hunter.
From above bright-billed whistlers, prudent scurry of lapwings,
The great quiet he brought me.

Excitement he gave me, where only
The sun's thought stirred to lyrics of warmth,
Crackle of gorse that was ripe on escarpments,
Hosting of rushes in their dream of blue sky.
When the imagination wakens, who calls
Rise up and walk, dance, look at the world?
Who is it hiding in the midst of the words
That were there on Flower Meadow Field and Flower Field?

And when the big clouds, the fugitive pilgrims,
Were red with the sunset of stormy November,
Down where the ashtrees and maples divided the fields,
The song of the wind was deep like deep silence.
Who, in the midst of the pomp, the super-abundance,
Stands there inviting, containing it all?
Each witness's witness, each memory's memory, life of each life,
Quiet calmer of the troubled self.

Till at last the whole world came into the stillness
And on the two fields his people walked,
And through, and between, and about them, goodwill widened
And rose out of hiding, to make them all one,
As when the few of us forayed with pitchforks
Or from heavy meadows lugged thatching of rush,
How close we came then, one to another –
The quiet huntsman so cast his net round us!

Ages of the blood on the grass and the light of grief,
Who whistled through them? Who heard but the heart?
The cheater of pride, and every trail's tracker,
Escaper from the armies, hey, there's his whistling –
Knowledge of us, knowledge, till at last we do know him!
Great was the leaping of hearts, after their ice age.
The fountains burst up towards heaven, till,
Falling back, their tears were like leaves of a tree.

Day broods on all this beneath sun and cloud,
And Night through the cells of her wide-branching brain –
How quiet they are, and she breathing freely
Over Flower Meadow Field and Flower Field –
Keeps a grip on their object, the field full of folk.
Surely these things must come. What hour will it be
That the outlaw comes, the hunter, the claimant to the breach,
That the Exiled King cometh, and the rushes part in his way?

Translated from the Welsh of Waldo Williams   b. 1904

The deluge, 1939 (extract)

From Merthyr to Dowlais the tramway climbs,
A slug's slime-trail over the slag heaps.
What's nowadays a desert of cinemas,
Rain over disused tips, this once was Wales.
Pawnshops have closed their doors. Clerks
Of the labour exchange are the chiefs of this prairie.
All flesh has tainted its way on the face of the earth.

The same taint's in me, as I second proposals
In committee after committee, to bring the old land to life.
I'd maybe be better employed on a Tonypandy corner
And my eyes meditating up the valley and down
On the human wreckage adrift in the mire of despond,
One function common to man and the standing slag.

Eyes have been changed to dust, we know not our death,
Were buried by our mothers, had Lethe milk to drink.
We cannot bleed, no, not as former men bled,
Our hands would resemble a hand, if they'd thumbs to go on them.
If a fall shatters our feet, all we do is grovel to a clinic,
Touch our caps to a wooden leg, Mond pension and insurance:
Knowing neither language nor dialect, feeling no insult,
We gave our masterpiece to history in our country's M.P.s.

Translated from the Welsh of Saunders Lewis   b. 1893

Herbert Williams   b. 1933

The old tongue

We have lost the old tongue, and with it
The old ways too. To my father's
Parents it was one
With the *gymanfa ganu*, the rough
Shouts of seafarers, and the slow
Dawn of the universal light.
It was one with the home-made bread, the smell
Of cakes at missionary teas,
And the shadows falling
Remotely on the unattempted hills.

It is all lost, the tongue and the trade
In optimism. We have seen
Gethsemane in Swansea, marked
The massacre of innocents. The dawn
Was false and we invoke
A brotherhood of universal fear.
And the harbour makes
A doldrum of the summer afternoon.

Even the hills are diminished.
They are a gallon of petrol,
There and back. The old salts
Rot. And the bread
Is tasteless as a balance sheet.

Oh yes, there have been gains.
I merely state
That the language, for us,
Is part of the old, abandoned ways.

And when I hear it, regret
Disturbs me like a requiem.

Depopulation

They say this is no place for the ambitious.
The young men leave, trailing
A pity for the people left behind,
Nailing the coffin of the town they go,
Finding refreshment in familiar lies.

And far from the accustomed hills they build
The structure of success which they were told
Would monument their paragon advance,
If only they were bold enough to leave
The moment they were old enough to go.

So now this is no place for the ambitious.
With every decade it is more
Conclusively a place which people leave
The moment they are bold enough to go.

And some have no regrets. But others find
A virtue in the ruin left behind,
And long to verify the truths
Their fathers read, and tread
The ways that scored their rooted enterprise,
And nurture a simplicity, until
A darkness comes to cover up their eyes.

But ambitious they are, ambitious to a man,
Made ambitious by their education,
Prisoners of their nourished talents.

So they display the customary
Pity for the people left behind.
But their bleak hearts speak
The bitter language of the dispossessed.

Jones the grocer

Jones the grocer, we called him –
A pale man, skilled in servility,
His hands white and soft as the lard he stacked
In small, meticulous rows, his head
Polished and somehow apologetic, as if
He was crowned forever with dishonour.

I hated him, he was too obsequious by far,
Embellishing transactions with fulsome flattery
Of your habits, your appearance, your miserable opinions.
He seemed to exist in a fog
Of self-effacement, through which one caught
The rarest glimpse of a human dignity.

Yet one could suffer the arid washing of his hands
For the joy of that shop, its curiosities,
Like the corner where it was always dusk
And equatorial, aromatic with coffee beans,
And the calendars derisive of topicality,
And the adverts twenty years out of date.

One could suffer it, and gladly suffer it again
To be delivered of this, its successor –
A supermarket, slick and soulless,
Arrogantly accepting the shoppers' homage.

The aliens

They brought a foreign warmth
To valleys bleak with strife
And Calvinism, brewing
A relaxation in the coffee cups.
And sunny voices learned
The mysteries of a tongue
Dark with the shadows of an ancient war.
They read the native ways
But kept, perhaps, an irony
Hidden behind their friendly, Latin eyes.
But they were too polite
To mock our self-denial,
And anyway, it wasn't good for business.

Their cafés, innocent
Of obvious sin, were yet
Viewed with disapproval by the folk
Who idolized a God
Who never smiled on Sunday,
And thunderously visited a curse
On all who stepped inside
To buy a box of matches for
A pipe of surreptitious Sabbath peace.
And yet the cafés spread.
And they became accepted.
And God, at last, was able to relax.

Times change. Some chapels now
Are turned to supermarkets,
The gospel is according to demand.
And hedonistic clubs
Have striptease on a Sunday,
Behind the seventh veil lies the promised land.
But still the Rabaiottis,
Bracchis and Antoniazzis
Keep their faith in God intact
And their attitude polite:
The customer, of course, is always right.

Epitaph

He was in no sense an eminent man.
Nobody fêted him at the Savoy,
Measured his profits, or even
Tossed him an O.B.E. He lived
Strictly in anonymity, save
For a certain local reputation
In the art of understanding Government documents,
And helping the bewildered
To claim a crumb from organized Mammon.

He was proud of this skill. He was not,
In the finest sense, modest. He would speak
Complacently of how he refused
A drink among drinkers, and was
Admired for it. You may condemn this
Parading of virtue, but why let it vex you?
He was, after all, unworthy of notice,
He was in no sense an eminent man.

And yet I remember his
Passion for knowledge, the way he
Pursued it in the earnest manner of the humble:
Penny readings, night classes,
University extension lectures – these
Were his curriculum. And he never
Rebelled against learning, although his bread
Was rarely more than formally buttered.
It was, for him,
Reward in itself, not a means
Of immediate grace and material glory.

And now the dust stops his mouth, and worms
Deride his dignity, I recall
His affection for children, the happy
Knack of his laughter, and the way
He would hoist his cap and shout 'Great Scotland Yard!'
I remember how he made failure
An honoured possession. And I feel
An indignation with death, although I expect
No-one to share it. For triumphantly I declare it –
Save for the mighty love he inspired,
He was in no sense an eminent man.

John Ackerman Jones   b. 1934

Cyprus, 1958

I know that I should talk and talk
Of the necessary victories and sing
A noisy epic, how sacrifice
Must path a return of spring
Before the new green towers to the sky.
I admit, too, it is useless to question why.

I know that I should speak of a battle,
And see two sides fighting for amity.
Telling how statesmen cannot turn the key
Until the door is forced.
I know it is important that they boast
A victory, and the dead hang
Like Christmas presents from the trees.

I know I should celebrate a military glory,
Poets have many times fashioned this story:
The elegy of victory, the triumphant state
Whilst the second bites the dust.
But I can think only of an old man
Reverent with age, groping
Before a shell-pocked home.
His silvered hairs expect no second dawn.
Beside him, in the cool shadow of this cypress,
A mother, her loves as tattered as her dress,
Grieves a husband and son,
Her foot kicking their dead leaves.
A child cries by an open door.
The victors may do as they please.

Forgive me if I do not try to catch
The march and colour of your battle song.
My gaze cannot reach past the boy
Sprawled in the sun, his gun, like a toy
Cast indifferently aside.

Because it hurt so much he died.
I think, for he was young,
At the last he cried and swore
While, like a fiery spring,
The red blood bubbled from his lung.
I cannot see whose insignia he wore.
Only his black hair flutters in the morning breeze,
A gentle sun, no bullets now, divides the trees.

I know that I should talk and talk,
But I am grown sick of the testimony
Of polite and politic men.

I leave the elegy and whitewash to them.

Bryn Griffiths   b. 1935

Talley Abbey

Here above the scattered stones of Talley Abbey, a bird bullets
Down the sky, drops down to die and stuns the clear air,
To where the lake lies dreaming in the still winter's day.

The eye, caught in the dark valley's timeless clutch,
Sees the twin worlds of air and water work once more –
A finned and diving bird below the water's floor!

Talley, one great rising arch of forgotten faith,
Remains in mind, cross-nailed by time, in the years
That wheel from childhood to the final darkness of our fears.

Five centuries away from sainthood, God's one boxed room
Of blind prayer stands, stone on stone, under the blasphemy of birds,
By the waiting water where no faith will ever burn again!

A sadness slumbers here in lake and dumb gray wall –
All signs of sanctity gone in the work of weather, man and bird –
Challenged only by the cry of creatures feathered, finned, and furred.

The lake remains, stones winter crack and fall, and Wales
Lives on in the stunted men who walk her lanes and lonely hills . . .
The memoried nets sieve still and only the dogma kills.

The old land creaks on in heave of mountain, crack of furrow,
Where this race and their speech stubborn the tide of history
As the nightwind cries along the lakeside and stirs the water's face.

And now, here above lake and abbey, another, soaring, bird
Spins in the trawled sky over Talley; and only a dog's distant bark
Disturbs the valley's silence and the slow dusk of Mabinogion dark.

Dying at Pallau

I remember him now as he was then,
Lying near death in the creaking house,
On that wild night in Wales

When the wind stole breath and the bombing rain
Beat against the farmhouse windows –
Beat through the surf of rushing trees
Where the tides of darkness spilled and ran
Over the drowned fields . . .
And his children, come again to his side,
Praying away the waters of his death.

Tom Davies of Pallau: farmer and man;
Eighty-seven years in this cage of toil;
Deacon and teacher of the green and country crafts
To the changing children, growing into peace.
He lay, willow-thin under the heavy quilts,
With all his death apparent
In a hand's thin bone; breathing harshly
With the pressure of his farming years.

Aye, I remember him that night –
His whispered Welsh greeting as I came in –
Barely heard above the vast echo
Of the wind, and the rain exploding
On the room-reflecting window-panes –
And all the kindness living in his eyes
As he slowly died towards the attic of his days.

The old house lives on in the warring winds,
Creaking still in all the weathers of Wales,
Imbued with the memory of his life and gentle ways.

The master

You worked me well, Mr. Thomas.
Duw, mun, all that writing
About an old nobody like me . . .
Exposing me, Prytherch, like that.
Jawl! Who would have believed it, mun –
Asking all those old questions all the time,
Ordering me about, just about,
And never believing anything I said . . .

That day when you came down
From Moel y Llyn and asked me
(In Welsh, of course)
If I ever realized the drabness
Of my stark environment –
Whatever that meant –
And the meaning of my life,
And you a vicar, too.

Well, now, Mr. Thomas, I've never
Really given it much thought, you see –
I mean there's the farm to look after,
The milking, and the sheep to tend,
And one doesn't get much time
For other things. But I've fine company,
You know: Sian's a good dog,
A good friend.

You did push me a bit hard at times,
Mr. Thomas, and tired me with talk,
But I don't really gob much, you know,
And I didn't care much for you saying
Of my 'half-witted grin'.
I'm not dull. I go to the *eisteddfodau*
And I know all about *englynion* –
And what more do I need than that?

You're in your world and I'm in mine.
I don't go to church, you see –
Chapel's good enough for me!
(And you making the village
Work to your words . . .)
I mean, who are you to talk?
Up there, high and mighty in your vicarage,
Playing the lord in Eglwys Fach.

The stones remember

Only the stones remember.
Only the stones have seen all the dead
season spinning into darkness;
walls and forests reaching high,
and then crumbling, dying,
withering to become one
with the worn land again.
Standing stones litter this landscape.
In this part of Wales
their lichened masses serve
as locking stones in clogged hedges;
form clumsy gateposts
for crossed webs of creaking wood;
or they stand alone in silent fields,
leaning back like the wind-battered
trees of this land. Like the people here,
a people growing old,
their very silence nudges
the stranger to a vague knowledge of guilt.

This is the word's frontier,
a place of hewn silence,
but sometimes, near the stones,
I almost hear a far singing
sounding from the past's distance –
a chanting of strange ritual
that bells soft and clear.

I am part of this country.
A single stone tells me
of countless forefathers who sang
and conquered here; tells me
of the stored centuries that still live,
shadowing the land like drifting clouds
under a sun grown old.
I cannot break free, sever the blood's shackle,
for each time I pass through this country,
this torn and weathered canvas
of mountain, forest and sea,
the cragged terrain harries me
with a spectral sense of the past
that is not memory
but a felt heritage of the ages.

Trefdraeth

It seems that no clear future
can exist in this place:
only the past hangs like mountain cloud,
echoing the lost days, stirs
in the town that appears to be slowly
sliding down the hill towards the sea.

Trefdraeth, town on the shore,
once the gray stone home
of the invading Norman and Saxon
who won but were lost in this harsh landscape;
buried in a race darker and older
than even the fair Celt,
who also came conquering here.

The Normans, as usual, built
their grim walls of massive stone;
granted charters and the right
for men to be serfs under their hand;
and then they sank out of sight
into the Iberian sea that surrounded them.

Conquest, the iron weight of arms,
only ended in their defeat
by the slow siege of assimilation.
Only the Celts, bright-haired islands
in this swarthy sea, survived and achieved
some measure of victory –
settled the singing pattern

of their language on the small frame
of the older race . . . But now
that same tongue is threatened, again,
from the East: from England they flood –
a cold warfare of tourists –
to stare and wonder, never to understand,

for one moment, our strangeness, or the way
our minds mull over an intricate phrase.
They depart at summer's ending, but
the following year finds them returning,
flocking like starlings, greedy to possess –
ruthless in a war of brandished banknotes –
to buy the cottages, small farms, the land itself.

Is it strange, then, that poverty
and the centuries of frugality,
this country's old attrition of need,
has weakened the Welsh here
to the point of final retreat
that lies in selling the land's heritage?

These people are strong still,
capable of endless and devious defence,
but the fear rings that *now*
English affluence, at last, will accomplish
what the force of arms failed to do –
and win this war of slow ages.

Peter Gruffydd   b. 1935

Macsen Wledig to the Welsh

Well, I knew they were foolish.
After all, did I not warn them
That my tiny chair held two
Not a whole gaggle of swish
Scholars and a failed people
Whose din breaks my heart in the moo
And baa of their weeping?

Ah, my people, in your keeping –
What? a fingerhold on Dafydd,
A conviction of the past, a whorish
Twilight of dreams; that, with
Your lack of courage, is seeping
Up your marrow-bones: clownish
How you wail and weep!

Ah, my people, can you not keep
Your inheritance amongst you?
The scars, you say, lie deep;
And how diligently you reopen the blue
Old wounds, living on your ancient wrongs.
Man, go wail in Annwn and beat gongs
To muddle yourselves more.

I cannot be ashamed again.
That is past now and the ore
(As your scholars say to gain
Understanding with their eyes shut)
Of your loded history is mined away.
Fact that you listen to me shows the hut
Where you are hid, the past; turn and face day.

Shepherd

Time had spaced the air with infrequent
Jags of rock and the ground was quick
With boulders and ideas of years past.
The capped and mufflered shepherd and two dogs
Were granite over the wambling sheep.
The peace of eagles brooded on the crags.

Sharply, to the sudden, shrill peep
Of the man's tongue, one of the furred blocks
Snaked over the wizened grass and, free
From the weight of time which dog and man
Felt in their stiffening bones, harried the leisurely
Sheep, cropping the brown and bents of the hill.

Here the trio were master; but in the lorried
Town they slipped and dodged on the roads, like
Their sheep, chivvied by the oil and noise
Of traffic: what caught them into our time?
Nothing, except the pressure of mortality.

The wind withers, the years drown on the rain rocks
As the sheep mortgage the dwindling grass.
Over them hoods the blankness of the wasted,
Even though fair and sunset, sky;
And the still vigilance of man and dog.

The small nation

Yet there are few things small in you,
Except that vital tree—courage.
Your poets scourge you and, with each
Crack of rage, you bow further
Into the dirt. All the scaly ways
Of selling are scored in your
Present face, the snivelling cares
Of profit and loss, the sad slow
Dimension of death darkening
The dull years leading to the end.

No register but the lean bone,
The gratuitous thanks for the unfelt
Insult, the sclerosis of the soul,
Can be scanned with any honesty.
What shall men do, wrapped
In your dark nets of subterfuge?
Some are imprisoned, to gnaw
Anew in solitude the dry bone
Of their love, but the rest of us
Are free, for various practical reasons.

No past's mounted trophies
Can do more than induce
A sentimental groan. There is now
No bugle of words to tap
A well of truth, nothing –
But the tarmac'd road
Past the supermarkets
And the tarred vowels
Of a tongue abrasive as thistles.

No blood suffices and we attend
The slow funeral of a small nation:
In the end there will be silence;
Now, even the withered heart rages.

Sally Roberts   b. 1936

Beginning

I can't see the stars;
Only a blackbird in the garden,
Singing his heart out in the rowan tree,
Sings to a rising moon.

Here I'm alone,
Not lonely for thinking of you,
Spinning a sort of dream
Without an end.

Blackbird and I,
Both in the springtime singing,
Singing for love,
For dreams, for the chance of spring.

You, love, and I,
And the blackbird in the garden,
Drowned in the rowan tree
And the rising moon.

Metamorphosis

Gwion, cooking of salmon
For Ceridwen's son,
Was burnt on the finger
By the spluttering juice.

And sucking the wound
Was made prince of the secret stars,
Rhymer and madman,
Caught in a crazy year.

But if he had not
Tasted the mortal fish,
Refraining from sluttishness,
What should he become?

Better Ceridwen's gift
And her flailed wrath,
Better the swallowed seed
And the child in the water-ark.

A small tragedy

They came up in the evening
And said to him, 'Fly!
All is discovered!'
And he fled.

A quiet little man,
Of no importance.
In fifty years he had acquired
Only flat feet and spectacles
And a distressing cough.

After a month or more,
(He having gone so quickly)
An inspector called
And they began to find the bodies.

A large number of them,
Stuffed into cupboards and other corners.
(At work he was tidy,
But files and paper-clips
Are matters of some importance.)

In the end, of course,
He was hanged,
Very neatly,
Though pleading insanity.

A quiet little man,
Who knew what to do with files and paper-clips,
But had no ideas about people
Except to destroy them.

Country places, Mykonos

A saucer of liquid meant to kill the flies,
Tablecloth plastic, displaying a map of Greece,
Frames on distempered walls hold ancestors
Oddly sedate (just so were our parents once);
Sideboard (like one we had before, in Wales):
Slowly the foreign room becomes my own,
Mine the unordered clash of old and new,
Pine and mahogany, glass and the tawdry gloss
Of makeshift and imitation – only the heat is strange.
The heat – and a jar for water, curved to the shape
Of journeys and far-off endings, half unknown,
Troy and Mykene, Sparta and Thebes – the names
Hollow with too much speaking,
Symbolic of nothing now.

Lying here, then, flat on the lumpy bed,
Hearing the donkeys pass, the women call,
Hearing the water slop in the washing can,
Feet on the cobbled road, a baby fall –
Suddenly, as a word the mind repeats
Echoes an utter strangeness all at once,
So, to the eye, half-closed against the glare,
Shapes in the sunlight merge, transmute themselves,
Form and reform, a legend on the stone.
Dolphin of Delos, plunging a mile away,
Foams on the varnished wardrobe of my room,
Hooves on the cobbles are sheep in a northern street,
Vortigern's dragon dies where Apollo kills.

Light in the eyes – a spell to unite the worlds:
So much the same – outside are the rocks and the wind,
And a country that is not mine, not then or now,
Either by voice or kinship – and yet if I go,
Greeting involves me: I am a native here.

Peter Preece   b. 1936

Completion

Hollow is the wheatfield,
Empty in its yellow room;
Fallen is the heavy corn.

Machines run down
And their dust blows cold
But thick in the big loft
Is the grain,
Fat in its vast, gold swell.
A long-table supper
Sits in the kitchen,
Ready with its glasses
For the time-stretched men:
And a cross is waiting
For their calendar.

In this green-born moment
Of a season's song
Is the ripe unfolding
Of a long amen.

Alun Rees   b. 1937

Release John Lucifer!

It's time they let the devil out of hell.
Remember how they threw him in the cell
and tossed away the key? And all because
he figured he could run the business well,
perhaps a little better than the boss.

This was the boy most likely to succeed.
'This is the kind of fellow that we need',
imagine heavenly civil servants saying.
But not the sort they wanted in the lead.
Yet even Pilate granted Christ a hearing.

Take-over bids for heaven happen once.
Angelic cops don't give a second chance.
The company directors called a squad
to clear the meeting. They were late for lunch,
and they were getting hungry. So was God.

Eros at the Tottenham Royal

Child big with wonder, filling your heart's soft centre
with sweet thick images of gowns and baubles,
pleasure my lies with your half-believing smile,
fluting your known responses in uneasy trebles.

Gangster of the soft glance, muscling in with a sway
on the racket of indifference, you strong-arm
me into compliance with a single laugh,
tickle desire till it cries like a thunderstorm.

Under soft April skies I would cherish you
in the spring's bowers, watching my freedoms fall
like unregretted pigeons after the long
tumultuous flight. O queen of the crowded dance-hall,

involve me in your lacquered majesty,
your politics of rouge, and never let
the bright lights of your eyes dim down and glow
in the city's darkness like lonely cigarettes.

I walk the pavements of your young enjoyment
and look for your heart's true house; inquisitive,
I log the numbers of the many doors,
stopping to knock and ask where you really live.

John Idris Jones b. 1938

Green country, Clwyd

Place is important on this globe
of furrows with troughs of memory
following our plough. Everywhere
there are fragments.
A mound of earth will make a stone, or Caesar.

The snow lies thick, hands-deep, worlds
lie in layers in one place. Look!
look to the mountains anew.
In the snow the smallest creatures leave their prints.

Snow to water, dust to dust. But water
might be frost, or floods. Change ends in
change. Give every thing a meaning, then
dirt is clay to the fist.

To Ioan Madog, poet, ancestor

Grandmother spoke of you
(As she lay, arthritic, in her bed)
As a large gay man,
A blacksmith who shaped hoops
For ships. Portmadoc built them,
So many you could dance from deck to deck
The moil of labour in your ears mixed
With the rich note of the native tongue.

Nain died, and Grandfather
Had seen before his death
The house he had built,
Over the water near Port,
And the garden he made for his lineage –
Each stone he had carried
And the soil he had rubbed through his hands –
Signed away, and later sold for profit.
The family, fallen apart, accommodated him
As distant harbours do a broken ship.

I have, my only remnant of the past's wreck,
A book of your *barddoniaeth*,
With Nain's writing, beside the *in memoriams*,
Telling of the dead, for me, in English.
And in the shaped and stormy lines
A couplet, once famous, lies in state,
Its echo in the chapels failing now.

Gwaed y groes a gŵyd y graith
Na welir moni eilwaith.

Although I speak a bastard Welsh
These words of yours, ancestor,
With their raging sadness,
Might be a foreign tongue
Whose cadence I know
But cannot translate.

Beside the estuary on a cold slope
Close to their former home
My grandparents lie buried.
The cost of the gravestones was finally shared.
One day I looked for Taid's grave
But no stone then announced it.
Having failed, I stood on the long grass,
Looked through the trees and over the choppy water
To the town famous for sea-captains
And the legend of Madog
Who sailed, before Columbus, for the New World.

In Port, proud ships point no more
Their carved bows towards distant seas.
A boat steams in occasionally
With raw material for the explosives works.
The week-end sailing-boats are slim and haughty.
The wood has rotted, the mud has won,
And dogs roam the abandoned quays.
Port is bilingual, entertains tourists,
And on Sundays the young play tennis in the park.

The rich note fades:
The chapels loom;
The dirge seeps through the graven masonry.

Ni cheir diwedd
Byth ar sŵn y delyn aur.

So much is falling to ruin.
Let us hope, merely,
Ioan Madog,
Poet,
That time will leave us something of your song.

Meic Stephens   b. 1938

Old timers

for John Edwards

Look, there's Jenkin and his cronies
sunning themselves on the public seat,
old men in caps and faded macs, so
typical of all these valley towns that
you, stranger in our ramshackle midst,
might treat them with your local colour.

Then, since you have seen them thus,
others would hail the country's heroes
who match their wit and tall tales
about the time they marched to London
with banners, hymns, tight bellies,
red crusaders from the broken hills;

or, Bible and *Das Kapital* in pocket,
who fan the past into a living flame,
familiar with rebels, the Chartists
spiking bread and justice on a bloody
sheet, union men bossed from the pits,
Mabon and Keir Hardie in their day;

but, comrades in your far, green ease,
do not be simpled by glowing paint;
the picture has another perspective.
There is a blue scar on Jenkin's lung:
words, like steep hills, are beyond him,
he is buried alive with his memories.

Gomer saw the mine's small hell, but
flood, fall and explosion were nothing
to the bombardment of Mametz Wood:
he grins, still listening to the big guns,
his mind, like no man's land, riddled
with the barbed fantasies of war.

Llew had books in his front room
before the slump of 'twenty six: he
was the brightest lad in Heolgerrig
and touched his cap to no one; but
he picked his conscience to a scab
in queues for soup, employment, dole.

Dan had a *tyddyn* on Cefn Golau, ten
wet acres to hold his rooted heart;
today, the state's machines are there,
ripping coal from the obsolete soil:
his smooth sons settled for a tidy sum
that shocked the old man into silence.

Eyes, that could see the stubborn ewe
beyond the dog and long whistle, or
watch, by the light of a kitchen lamp,
an *englyn* carved like a lovespoon, now
observe, clouded with bewilderment,
the high street go about its business.

From terraces, flats and new estates
(Keir Hardie is the municipal slum),
our town is stricken by the crowd
that comes, this glittering morning,
to sport the slick rosettes of affluence
in supermarket, pub and betting shop;

while here, against the traffic's din
and posters selling petrol, sex and soap,
your heroes sit in the canvas sun
and mark the deadbeat time, eloquent
as the standing shafts, the spectral slag,
the great furnaces thick with bracken.

We do well to mark them now, each
in his way, for these are our fathers,
John, who have no future but in us.

Ponies, Twynyrodyn

Winter, the old drover, has brought
these beasts from the high moor's *hafod*
to bide the bitter spell among us,
here, in the valley streets.
Observe them, this chill morning, as
they stand, backsides against the wind,
in Trevithick Row. Hoofs, shod with ice,
shift and clatter on the stone kerb.
Steam is slavering from red nostrils,
manes are stiff with frost and dung.

Quiet now, last night
they gallivanted through the village,
fear's bit in teeth. Hedges were broken,
there was havoc to parked cars. Yet,
despite the borough council's by-laws,
these refugees are welcome here.
Fed from kitchen and tommybox, they
are free to roam the grit backlanes,
only kids and mongrels pester them.

We greet them as old acquaintances
not because they bring us local colour,
as the tourist guides might say, but
for the brute glamour that is with them.
Long before fences and tarmac, they
were the first tenants of these valleys,
their right to be here is freehold.

Now, in this turncoat weather, as
they lord it through the long terraces,
toppling bins from wet steps, ribs
rubbing against the bent railings,
our smooth blood is disturbed
by *hiraeth* for the lost *cantrefi*,
the green parishes that lie beyond
the borders of our town and hearts,
fit for nothing now but sad songs.

These beasts are our companions,
dark presences from the peasant past,
these grim valleys our common *hendre*,
exiles all, until the coming thaw.